The
NEW AGE
of
POLITICAL REFORM

The
NEW AGE
of
POLITICAL REFORM

The Electoral College,
the Convention,
and the Party System

Alexander M. Bickel

HARPER COLOPHON BOOKS
HARPER & ROW, PUBLISHERS
NEW YORK, EVANSTON, AND LONDON

THE NEW AGE OF POLITICAL REFORM. *Copyright © 1968 by Alexander M. Bickel. Printed in the United States of America. All rights reserved. No part of this book may be used or reproduced in any manner whatsoever without written permission except in the case of brief quotations embodied in critical articles and reviews. For information address Harper & Row, Publishers, Incorporated, 49 East 33rd Street, New York, N.Y. 10016. Published simultaneously in Canada by Fitzhenry & Whiteside, Limited, Toronto.*

FIRST EDITION

LIBRARY OF CONGRESS CATALOG CARD NUMBER: 69–17174

Contents

Contents

Cautions for Reformers

THE AMERICAN political system may be at a point of significant mutation, as it has not been since the first decade of this century. The Progressive Era of sixty years ago gave us women's suffrage and the popular election of Senators, without which the federal government would surely now seem hopelessly anachronistic; the direct primary, which has become a domesticated household creature; and also the initiative, the referendum, and the recall, which have survived here and there, but for the most part wildly, in a state of nature, owing to lack of regular contact with humans. These reforms answered essentially to the populist impulse. The populist idea, identified in the American political tradition with Andrew Jackson and in some measure with everyone else ever since, is that the ills of society and its government will be cured by giving a stronger and more certain direction of affairs to a popular majority. Today as earlier, this remains the battle cry of reform. It alone inspired the Supreme Court's reapportionment decisions from 1962 onward, which may be viewed either as having inaugurated the current age of political reform or as a reflection of it; and it alone is the overt inspiration of proposals, for which the performance of the system this season has generated much support, to abolish the electoral college and the Presidential nominating conventions.

Confidence in the majority crosses class and ideological lines; nearly everyone believes that if the majority were but allowed to speak often and loudly enough, it would speak with his own voice. And ultimately, in one or another degree, everyone must so believe. Even for those who would try to control the processes by which a majority is formed and who would restrain and educate the majority before yielding to its wishes, the democratic faith is, finally, faith in the good will and good sense of the preponderant number of men. But the unqualified populist principle is simplistic and insufficient. Over time, it begets a dialectic of illusion and disillusion. Its sanguine slogans sound hollow and become terms of derision with extraordinary rapidity. "The Old Order Changeth," wrote William Allen White in 1910. In 1920, he said to Ray Stannard Baker: "What a God-damned world this is! . . . If anyone had told me ten years ago that our country would be what it is today . . . I should have questioned his reason."

The proclamation of a New Politics will also be recalled in irony later if it is given none but a populist content now. It is nice to think that there is an immediate majority out there which necessarily favors great good works, and which consists of persons each moving in an individual orbit, adrift from parties and other structures, and yet capable of exercising power if only every man had one vote. But the body politic is not like that. Majorities do not arise spontaneously and are not found; they must be constructed and then maintained. They are conglomerates of many groups, all of them minorities, each of which must have its share of power, some of which weigh in with intensity of feeling rather than numbers, and some of which must sometimes even be granted a veto, in order that there may be peaceable government enjoying common consent. If this is the Old Politics, it is the part of it which is a permanent necessity.

Unqualified populists or not, political reformers must in any case proceed with caution. James I spoke of the mystery of the King's power. The institutions of a secular, democratic government do not generally advertise themselves as mysteries. But they are. What they do, how they do it, or why it is necessary to do what they do is not always outwardly apparent. Their actual operation must be assessed, often in sheer wonder, before they are tinkered with, lest great expectations be not only defeated, but mocked by the achievement of their very antithesis. Defeat and mockery, to assert briefly what is common knowledge, were the partial result of the direct primary, and certainly of the referendum, the initiative, and the recall, which turned into tools of minority pressure; and defeated expectations and unwanted consequences, to assert briefly what will in time also be common knowledge, have followed from the Supreme Court's reapportionment decisions.[1]

There are great virtues in a conservative attitude towards structural features of government. The sudden abandonment of institutions is an act that reverberates in ways no one can predict, and many come to regret. There may be a time when societies can digest radical structural change, when they are young and pliant, relatively small, containable, and readily understandable; when men can watch the scenery shift without losing their sense of direction. We are not such a society. We are well served by an attachment to institutions that are often the products more of accident than of design, or that no longer answer to their original purposes and plans, but that offer us the comfort of continuity, and challenge our resilience and inventiveness in bending old arrangements to present purposes with no outward change. The English know this secret, and so does the common law that we inherited from them.

We have, of course, many institutions and arrangements that, as they function, no longer conform to the original scheme, and we have bent most of them quite effectively to

[1] See, e.g., Robert G. Dixon, Jr., *Democratic Representation: Reapportionment in Law and Politics* (New York: Oxford University Press, 1968), pp. 17–18, 21–22, 574–581.

the purposes of our present society, which in all respects differs enormously from the society of nearly two hundred years ago. The Supreme Court is one such institution, and the Presidency itself is another. The fact that we have used them without modifying their structures has lent stability to our society and has built strength and confidence in our people.

2

The Electoral College

THE "HUMPTY DUMPTY electoral college," as one of its critics has called it, is another old institution put to interesting new uses. Now the chief target of reformers, the electoral college was unquestionably invented to serve ends we no longer care to serve, and which it no longer serves. Only in form does it remain what it was invented to be. Pursuant to Article II of the Constitution and the Twelfth Amendment, it still consists of as many electors from each state as the state has Senators and Representatives, and it still convenes quadrennially to elect a President and a Vice-President of the United States. (See Appendix I.) But although it was probably intended, and clearly not forbidden, to act independently, it has not done so, at least not in modern times. Electors compete for the office in a popular election, but with very infrequent exceptions, which have never proved significant, they do so in complete anonymity, being pledged to Presidential and Vice-Presidential candidates for whom, if they win by a majority or plurality, they cast their state's total electoral vote.

The Great Divide and Urban and Minority Power

These features of the system, unforeseen and unintended by its originators and dependent on custom, not on the Constitution, have bred in modern times the decisive influence in Presidential elections of the large, populous, heterogeneous states, where bloc voting, as by ethnic or racial minorities or other interest groups, often determines the result. Much of the popular vote in the smaller, relatively homogeneous states is simply wasted. Politicians and political scientists have at any rate long assumed that the Presidency is won or lost in the large states. It hardly mattered that no one was altogether sure, for the assumption governed the strategy of Presidential campaigns, and was thus self-validating.

Recently, however, Mr. John F. Banzhaf, III, has adduced mathematical proof. Using a computer, he has analyzed the various possible arrangements of electoral votes, and the circumstances in which any given state could change the result of an election. He has also calculated the chances of a voter affecting the outcome in his state and the chances that the outcome of a national election would then itself be altered. He has thus arrived at an estimate of the voting power of citizens of the several states, defining voting power—not unnaturally—as "simply the ability to affect decisions through the process of voting." And his conclusion is that voters in "states like New York and California have over two and one-half times as much chance to affect the election of the President as residents of some of the smaller states. . . ." Pennsylvania, Ohio, Michigan, Illinois, and even the lesser industrial states, are also in advantageous positions. The reason is that while a voter in a large state has a diminished chance of influencing the result in his state, because there are, of course, more people voting, he potentially influences a larger number of electoral votes, and so despite the apparent dilution of his vote, he actually exercises much greater control over the outcome of the national election. This power he derives directly from the electoral college system.[1]

So what we have known to be true is true. And we can now establish mathematically why modern Presidents have been particularly sensitive to urban and minority interests—

[1] See J. F. Banzhaf, III, "One Man, 3.312 Votes: A Mathematical Analysis of the Electoral College," *Villanova Law Review*, Vol. 13, No. 2 (Winter, 1968), pp. 303–346.

modern Presidents of both parties, this is to say, have been more responsive to urban interests than have other factions in their parties. And only men who can be so responsive are generally nominated and elected. Goldwater in 1964 is something of an exception; he was nominated. Mr. Nixon in 1968 was no exception. If he made some unfamiliar sounds, that was because of the particular urban mood of the day.

In modern times and in most of our politics, urban interests in the big states have contended against interests that have a more rural, nativist, and Protestant orientation. The latter interests have tended to dominate Congress, the former the Presidency. Urban-rural, pluralist-homogeneous—this has been the great divide in American politics. The task of the Presidential candidate, Republican or Democratic, is to bridge it from either side. The electoral college does not guarantee the Presidency to the Democrats. Rather the system requires both parties at least to make inroads in the urban and ethnic vote in order to win. Mr. Nixon in 1968 barely did, and he barely won. But then it was a three-way race, and some of the Wallace urban vote is to be credited to Nixon, either directly or as a subtraction from Humphrey strength. In any case, the industrial states were, as ever, the decisive battleground. The big states would matter in any scheme that took account of the popular vote in whatever fashion, directly or with qualifications. But the electoral college as it has evolved is so rigged that the big states count disproportionately. That is its critical attribute.

Each of our major parties is, in consequence, as James M. Burns has recently reminded us, two allied parties—a Congressional Party, rural and small-town, moderate to conservative in orientation, and a Presidential Party, which is substantially more urban liberal. (How often has it been true that the Republicans have lost Congress to the Democrats, and the urban liberals have lost the Democrats to Congress!) No doubt, the urban electorate is not always progressive, humane, and large-minded, and the more homogeneous rural and small-town electorate sometimes is. The drift of attitudes among big-city voters is nothing to be proud of just now, nor was it in the early 1950's. On the other hand, the Progressive movement of a half-century ago had deep roots in the rural West and Midwest. Still, the urban and the rural–small-town outlooks and interests do generally differ. And so long as that remains true, the former should exert particular influence through the Presidency because the latter are likely to prevail in Congress.

The difference in interest and outlook may not always obtain. The demography of the United States and its politics will not necessarily abide unaltered, world without end. The country, we are told, is increasingly urban, and TV and the other media are, God help us, leveling cultural and other distinctions. But "urban" is a term that can cover many ways of life, and the ethnic and racial composition—and traditions and attitudes—of an urbanized Nebraska or Georgia are still not quite those of New York, Chicago, Cleveland, and the like. If there are major changes in the offing they are not here yet, and their nature is not readily predicted. And when they come, will they not be digestible by the present system, as the great changes of the past have been? That is at least as probable as that we can know now how to alter the system so that it will suit us in circumstances dimly foreseen.

The proposal to abolish the electoral college that is now under active consideration emanated from a special committee set up by the American Bar Association,[2] and it has a very

---

[2] Robert G. Storey, dean emeritus of the Southern Methodist School of Law, was chairman. Members were: Senator Henry Bellmon, then Republican governor of Oklahoma; Professor Paul Freund, Harvard Law School; E. Smythe Gambrell of Atlanta, Georgia, a lawyer; Ed Gossett, former Democratic Congressman, of Dallas, Texas; William T. Gossett of Detroit, former general counsel of the Ford Motor Company; William I. Jameson,

great deal of bipartisan Congressional support. It has even spawned a thoroughly documented and well-argued book.[3] It calls for a constitutional amendment providing for election of Presidents and Vice-Presidents by nationwide popular vote, with a runoff in the event that no candidate attains a plurality of 40 per cent. (See Appendix II.) The idea is simple and attractive, and seems unarguably on the side of the angels. To resist it is to play Darwin and T. H. Huxley to the Bar Association's Disraeli. In commenting on the debate between certain divines, who claimed that man was a creature of God and kin to the angels, and Darwin and Huxley, who, of course, placed us on the family tree of the monkeys, Disraeli said, "My Lords, I am on the side of the angels." In the same sense, but so much more earnestly, without the saving grace of Disraeli's irony, the Bar Association and a whole lot of Senators and Congressmen are also on the side of the angels. However, as in the quarrel over the theory of evolution, there is another side.

The direct popular election would put a premium, not on carrying the two-party industrial states, but on achieving the largest possible majority in the smaller, more homogeneous ones. It would create a Presidency with little or no incentive to act as a counterweight to Congress, and as a particular spokesman for urban and minority groups. This, one may

---

a United States district judge in Montana; Kenneth B. Keating, the former Republican Senator from New York; Otto Kerner, then Democratic governor of Illinois; Professor James C. Kirby, Jr., of Northwestern University Law School; James M. Nabrit, Jr., president of Howard University; Herman Phleger of San Francisco, legal adviser to the State Department during the Eisenhower Administration; Professor C. Herman Pritchett of the University of Chicago political science department; Walter P. Reuther, president of the United Automobile Workers; and Whitney North Seymour of New York, a lawyer.

[3] Neil R. Peirce, *The People's President* (New York: Simon and Schuster, 1968).

reasonably surmise, is precisely what conservative backers of the proposal intend. One of its most ardent Congressional sponsors is Senator Everett M. Dirksen of Illinois. He knows who would be the gainers. His many liberal allies in this venture think they are outsmarting him. Mr. Dirksen is delighted with the prospect of altering the Presidential constituency while Congress continues to be what it is. Liberals would presumably hesitate to do that. Mesmerized, however, as Mr. Dirksen never has been, by the one man, one vote rhetoric, they say that Congress will not remain unchanged, and that no counterweight to it is needed, therefore, or is any longer proper—all because of the Supreme Court's reapportionment decisions. It was fitting for the President to be oriented toward the cities and minority groups so long as Congress looked the other way, the argument goes, but Congress looked the other way because of malapportionment, and malapportionment is no more. Hence the reasons, such as they were, for tolerating the undemocratic aberration of the electoral college no longer hold. It is time for the system to be ideologically pure. The Court has said that the Constitution commands equal apportionment. We should, therefore, reapportion the Presidency. In effect, we must now amend the Constitution to make it mean what the Supreme Court has said it means.

It is an arresting argument. But its paradoxical nature is not the main thing wrong with it. What is fundamentally wrong with it is that one may think a system of countervailing centers of power better for a country as large and still as diverse as ours than one in which Congress and the President represent more nearly the same constituency. One may think that under the present system we are able to strike a nice balance in our government, and make it an instrument for achieving general consent, rather than merely for working the will of some supposed majority of the moment; and that, therefore, instead of changing the Constitution so as to conform it to the Supreme Court's reapportionment decisions, we ought to work to overturn those decisions.

Even if one accepts the reapportionment decisions and their exclusively majoritarian bias, however, the trouble is that the proponents of the popular election wildly overestimate their immediate impact and their durability. The reasons are many. It is, to begin with, impossible without additional constitutional amendment entirely to reapportion the House. State lines prevent. Secondly, it is foolhardy to bank on the permanence of the reapportionment decisions, just exactly as we now know them. They are subject to relitigation every decade, with every census. Third, gerrymanders, which the Court has not yet attempted to control, can accomplish all that the most sophisticated or antiquated malapportionment ever achieved. Indeed, "a reliance on a fairly rigid standard for apportionment," writes Robert G. Dixon, Jr., "which requires maximum sacrifice of other considerations such as political subdivision groupings . . . can operate to maximize gerrymandering freedom."[4] But fourth and most important, we do not begin to know that Congress is what it is because of malapportionment. It is quite probable that in much larger measure the nature of Congress is determined by its internal methods of distributing power—chiefly the seniority and committee systems. These are very solidly entrenched. They reward length of service and expertise, as in one fashion or another all legislatures—really all permanent institutions—must. Long tenure is, in turn, most often the gift of a homogeneous district, which will tend also to liberate a Congressman from the varied concerns of a closely divided and diverse constituency, and thus enable him to specialize single-mindedly in a branch of legislative business. Congress may

[4] *Democratic Representation,* p. 18.

also, finally, be what it is because any districted constituency will vote differently for a Congressman, from a more restricted and probably more conservative perspective, than when it votes as part of the entire national constituency in Presidential elections. Herein may lie the explanation of a certain divergence between the Senate, itself atrociously malapportioned and proof against reform even by constitutional amendment, which is now elected by statewide popular vote, and the districted House of Representatives. This may mean that in any circumstances the President is fairly bound to represent a constituency that is not the same as that of the House, but it means more plainly that Congress cannot be radically changed by reapportionment and that the system should emphasize and preserve rather than seek to suppress the different orientation of the Presidency.

Two other suggestions, not now so seriously entertained as the proposal for popular election, go beyond merely shifting the orientation of the Presidency, and seek quite explicitly, and with the utmost precision, to merge its constituency with that of Congress. Both would retain the electoral college apportionment of voting power among the states, and thus the apparent bonus, as in the Senate, accruing to the small states. But they would translate the appearance of the present electoral college system into the reality of the Senate by abolishing the practice of casting a state's vote as a winner-take-all unit. One plan, long advocated by Republican Senator Karl E. Mundt of South Dakota, would cause two Presidential electors to be chosen at-large in each state, like its Senators, and the rest in Congressional districts. (See Appendix III.) In successfully opposing this idea in the Senate in 1956, John F. Kennedy said: "It is not only the unit vote for the Presidency we are talking about, but a whole solar system of governmental power. If it is proposed to change the balance of power of one of the elements of the solar system, it is necessary to consider the others."[5] The other plan, introduced as long ago as 1948 by Senator Henry Cabot Lodge, Republican of Massachusetts, and Representative Ed Gossett, Democrat of Texas, who more recently served on the American Bar Association committee that proposed popular election, would divide each state's electoral vote, apportioned as at present, in proportion to the popular one. (See Appendix IV.) This plan was actually passed in the Senate as a constitutional amendment in 1950 by the necessary two-thirds majority, but went down to ultimate defeat in the House. Mr. Gossett argued for it at one point as follows: "Is it fair, is it honest, is it democratic . . . to place such a premium [as the present system does] on a few thousand labor votes, or Italian votes, or Irish votes, or Negro votes, or Jewish votes, or Polish votes, or Communist votes, or big-city machine votes, simply because they happen to be located in two or three large, industrial pivotal states?" The premium placed on their votes, Mr. Gossett went on, had enabled Negroes to obtain promises of fair employment practices legislation in the major party platforms in 1944 and 1948, and the Jews to exact support for Zionist objectives.[6]

Either the districting or the proportional device could be adopted by state legislatures at any time (the districting device was, in fact, used in the early years, and by one state as late as 1832), since the practice of awarding the entire elec-

[5] Quoted in Peirce, *The People's President,* p. 159. John Kennedy also opposed the Lodge-Gossett Plan, mentioned next in the text, as well as popular election, although, to be sure, these are views he took before the reapportionment cases had been decided in the Supreme Court. See *ibid.,* pp. 172–173, 186. But in 1966, well after the reapportionment decisions, Robert Kennedy strongly opposed both the Mundt and Lodge-Gossett plans, and expressed serious doubts about popular election, too. See *Election of the President,* Hearings before the Subcommittee on Constitutional Amendments of the Senate Judiciary Committee, 89th Congress, 1st Session (1966), pp. 179–185.

[6] Quoted in Peirce, *The People's President,* pp. 169–170.

toral vote to the popular winner rests on custom. But most large states will not soon abandon the custom voluntarily, understanding that it works to their advantage, and so long as some states continue to cast a bloc electoral vote, it is unprofitable for the other ones not to. So the districting and proportional methods—or a choice between them—would have to be imposed by constitutional mandate. In 1966, Delaware and twelve other states sued to have the Supreme Court order universal adoption of one or the other method. They claimed that the winner-take-all custom is a form of malapportionment, as indeed in practice it is, although districting or proportional allocation of the electoral vote would merely substitute another sort of malapportionment, weighted in another way. As might have been expected, the plaintiffs in addition to Delaware were Arkansas, Florida, Iowa, Kansas, Kentucky, Oklahoma, North Dakota, South Dakota, Utah, West Virginia, and Wyoming—but also, surprisingly, Pennsylvania. The defendants were all the other states, with New York in the leading position. The Supreme Court had the good sense not to entertain the suit,[7] although conceivably the last has not been heard of this species of litigation.

Popular Election and the Two-Party System

There is a separate objection to the proposal for direct popular election—applicable in almost the same degree against the districting and proportional plans also—which would be entirely sufficient in itself. The monopoly of power enjoyed by the two major parties would not likely survive the demise of the electoral college. Now, the dominance of two major parties enables us to achieve a politics of coalition and accommodation rather than of ideological and charismatic fragmentation, governments that are moderate, and a regime that is stable. Without forgetting that of all the mysteries of

[7] *Delaware v. New York,* 385 U.S. 895 (1966).

government the two-party system is perhaps the deepest, one can safely assert that each major party exerts centripetal force; that it ties to itself the ambitions and interests of men who compete for power, discouraging individual forays and hence the sharply defined ideological or emotional stance; that it makes, indeed, for a climate inhospitable to demagogues; and that it provides by its very continuous existence a measure of guidance to the marginally interested voter who is eminently capable of casting his ballot by more irrelevant criteria. The system, in sum, does not altogether take mind out of politics, but it does tend to ensure that there are few irreconcilable losers, and that the winners can govern, even though—or perhaps because—there are equally few total victories. Multiparty systems also govern by compromise and coalition, of course; they compromise and coalesce, however, not before the election, but after, having first offered the voter his choice among pure positions. Self-contained ideologies thus take root, and become hard-edged. Accommodation is more difficult, partial, grudging, short-lived, and often impossible. Such a system makes for more mind, perhaps, and certainly less government.

The electoral college as it now operates deters challenges to the two major parties, because an effective challenge must have not merely some popular appeal, but support of sufficient regional concentration to garner an electoral vote. In 1912, William H. Taft, the real third-party candidate in the extraordinary circumstances of that year, had 23.2 per cent of the popular vote and 8 electoral votes, and in 1924 Robert M. LaFollette had 16.6 per cent, and 13 electoral votes. Only from a regional base can a third party penetrate the electoral college. Thus in 1948 Strom Thurmond had such a base, and Henry Wallace did not. Each got 2.4 per cent of the popular vote, but Thurmond had 39 electoral votes (31 more than Taft in 1912, with his 23.2 per cent) to Wallace's none. George Wallace last year also ran on about the only issue which still massively unites a region—hence his 45 electoral votes. Otherwise, his 13 per cent of the popular vote would have been as meaningless as Taft's 23 or LaFollette's 16.

Popular election would unquestionably invite nonregional interests that have failed to influence conventions to enter the general election in the hope of gathering enough votes to bargain with in a runoff. And enough entrants may be foreseen to ensure a runoff each time. The point can be illustrated by assuming an antiwar candidacy in 1968. With support distributed across the country, a popular vote of even as much as 25 per cent could well have resulted in very few electoral votes, or none. That is one reason why there was no such candidacy. Eliminate the electoral college, however, and an antiwar candidacy would have been eminently worth while, indeed essential. For the period between the first election and the runoff, rather than the national party convention as now, would be the coalition-forming stage. Every consideration that brought forth antiwar candidates for the Democratic nomination would with equal—and greater—validity have propelled an antiwar candidate into the general election.

The two major parties could not long sustain themselves in such conditions. We would see on a national scale the kind of unstructured politics that characterized much of the single-party South in its heyday. The real election was the Democratic primary, which would draw several candidates, who then sorted themselves out between the first vote and the runoff. Two or four years thence, everything started afresh.[8]

A geographically based candidacy such as that of George Wallace will have no less incentive to manifest itself under a system of popular election than now. All other possible separate candidacies, ideological but not regional, will have more, and they are surely going to be, as historically they have been, more typical.

[8] See V. O. Key, Jr., *Southern Politics* (New York: Alfred A. Knopf, 1949), pp. 406–423.

Minority Presidents

Apart from a theoretical attachment to pure majoritarianism, proponents of the direct popular election of the President rely also on a parade of possible horrible consequences of the present system. Both the electoral college and the direct popular election can produce plurality Presidents, who, like Mr. Nixon in 1968, came in ahead of their opponents by less than a majority of the total popular vote. The electoral college, however, can also bring a minority President into office, that is, one who got fewer popular votes than his runner-up. Yet putting aside an esoteric dispute about how to apportion the popular vote in Alabama in 1960, there has not been a minority President in this century; and in an election that was not stolen, as in 1876, or thrown into the House, as in 1824, there has been one only once in our history. And that was eighty years ago. But it made little difference that Grover Cleveland lost in 1888 even though he won by 100,000 votes, having won four years earlier, when he did become President, by 23,000. It would have made equally little difference if, without affecting the actual result in the electoral college, Mr. Nixon had nosed out John F. Kennedy in 1960 by 100,000 votes, or Mr. Humphrey had prevailed by a small margin in 1968. When some 70 million votes divide so closely, only an immensely dogmatic majoritarianism would insist that the so-called winner has the sole legitimate claim to office. In truth, there is a stand-off, and the question is merely of a convenient device—any convenient device previously agreed upon—for letting one of two men govern.

Unquestionably, the legitimacy of the electoral college result and the effective discharge of the office would be affected should the loser of the popular vote by a substantial margin win the Presidency. But of this, as past statistics consistently show, the risk is minuscule, and it is offset by the advantage of the electoral college in the more likely case of a close popular vote. For in the electoral college, a narrow popular victory is perceived through a magnifying glass.

Even if it should put a narrow loser in office, the electoral college would probably ensure greater acceptance for him than the winner by a very small margin could expect in a system of direct popular election. It is a statistical universe we inhabit, moreover, and it will continue to be, no matter how we elect our Presidents. Direct popular election comes equipped, as Professor Ernest J. Brown of the Harvard Law School has stressed, with its own brand of statistical nightmare. Suppose the popular-vote result is close, as in 1960 and 1968, or there are charges of error or fraud, as in 1876. At present, with the result magnified in the electoral college, the charges are most often immaterial, since most often the reassignment of some popular votes would not change the outcome. If it would, a recount or perhaps litigation may be called for in one or two states. But if the entire national popular vote is decisive, the recount in a close election might have to be nationwide. Would it be complete by January 20? The existing system, Professor Brown has written, "isolates and insulates charges of voting irregularities." Popular election might necessitate "re-examination of every ballot-box and voting machine in the country, not to mention also the records of registration and qualification of voters."[9]

Deadlock

Besides electing a minority President, which it is not apt to do, the electoral college is capable of two other tricks, both of which George C. Wallace has badly frightened people with. Since the Constitution permits the college to act as an independent, deliberative body, individual electors may take it

[9] E. J. Brown, "Proposed Amendment a Power Vacuum for Political Blackmail," *Trial* (June–July, 1967), pp. 15, 16.

into their heads to behave accordingly, and should no one have a majority of electoral college votes, some uncommitted or third-party electors could certainly play a decisive role. Obviously they should not, since they are obscure men who were not elected to perform a deliberative function. This is an eventuality that should be guarded against, but it calls for perfecting the present system, not for abandoning it. The Johnson Administration proposed a constitutional amendment which would abolish the electors and their college as a physical entity, and would automatically award the total electoral college vote of each state, calculated as at present, to the winner of a majority or plurality of the popular vote. (See Appendix V.)

A difficulty of rather another sort, and one not so easily solved, is the deadlock. The Constitution now provides that should no one succeed in obtaining a majority in the electoral college, the House of Representatives shall elect a President, each state having one vote, to be cast in accordance with the wishes of a majority of that state's delegation in the House. One may think it unlikely that patriotic men, committed in virtually every other aspect of their activities to majoritarian principles, would do today what was done in 1824, and elect, not the winner of the popular vote by a substantial plurality, but his runner-up; and if the margin between the two were narrow, or if as in 1824 a firm governing coalition were formed between candidates who together did have a plurality of the popular vote, one might think the result theoretically proper, or one may be indifferent to it in point of principle. Nevertheless, the possibility of intolerable abuse exists, and there is no reason not to guard against it. One suggestion, put forward by Representative Jonathan Bingham of New York, is to have a runoff election still within the electoral college system—that is, a repetition between the two top candidates of the previous exercise. (See Appendix VI.) This has some of the disadvantages of the popular election proposal with its runoff, since it might also tend to make splinter candidacies more profitable and hence more likely. Another possibility, favored by the Johnson Administration, is to recognize frankly that in the event of a deadlock a choice is required through a deliberative process, rather than through a process—which by hypothesis has just failed—of registering the popular wish. I shall touch presently in some detail on the coalition-making that precedes the general election in the present system. Deadlock means that it has failed and must be tried again. Coalition-making is a function for representative, deliberative institutions. Congress sitting in joint session and reaching decisions by a majority of the individual votes of its members is the best available deliberative institution for this purpose at such a time, and Congress is the institution the Johnson Administration proposal would use. (See Appendix VII.)

3

The National Party Convention

CONGRESS—that is to say, caucuses of members of each party in Congress—was the instinctive, initial choice of an institution to perform the function of building coalitions prior to the general election. Congressional caucuses nominated Presidential candidates until the system broke down in 1824. It did so because what had been for a time the single dominant Jeffersonian Party was itself breaking up, and because the caucus seemed insufficiently representative. The convention has been with us since 1832. Now it, too, seems insufficiently representative, and also inadequately deliberative.

More and more the convention appears, like the electoral college, merely to register the previously expressed wishes of a constituency, as the increasing incidence of first ballot nominations plainly suggests. What that constituency is, however, whether it is in any sense the masses of party adherents, or merely the professional party cadre, is gravely in question. No one can say for certain that Rockefeller rather than Nixon was the choice of the relevant body of voters who in 1968 constituted—or would have constituted—the Republican Party, or that McCarthy rather than Humphrey was the equivalent Democratic choice. But at least the Democratic Convention notably failed to convince one of the opposite. And so the majoritarian reformers would substitute a national primary election for the convention.

National Primaries and the Two-Party System

A national primary would undoubtedly attract numerous candidates, and its decisive stage would be the runoff. (See

Appendix VIII.) Consequently, as Nelson Polsby and Aaron Wildavsky have written, "the United States might have to restrict its Presidential candidates to wealthy athletes. No man without enormous financial resources could ever raise the millions required for the nominating petition, the first primary, the run-off primary, and the national election; and no one who was not superbly conditioned could survive the pace of all these campaigns."[1] Polsby and Wildavsky argue also that a national primary would badly strain the two-party system, because in periods of the dominance of one of the parties, which do occur, voters would be drawn to that party's primary, viewing it as their only real opportunity to participate decisively in the entire electoral process, and they would be drawn in such unnaturally large numbers as to threaten the other party with atrophy. In any event, a national primary would not avoid the coalition-building function, which must be discharged, whether before or after the general election. The consequence would be merely that the function would be de-institutionalized. Between the first primary and the runoff, men would come together, without structure and without form, and sort out their support for one of the two candidates who had emerged in the leading positions. This would be the time and this would be the fashion of the coalition-forming process in each party, and ultimately, if Polsby and Wildavsky are right, in one party alone, as—again—in the once-solid South.

Of course, if Polsby and Wildavsky are right, the general election would be a formality of little moment, and we would have the least desirable of all systems of direct popular election, one that provides for no prior nominating process of any sort. It would amount to a multi-party system, in which the bargaining that is essential for constituting a government is

[1] Nelson W. Polsby and Aaron B. Wildavsky, *Presidential Elections* (Scribner's, 2nd ed.; New York: 1968), pp. 229ff.

postponed until after the election. The disadvantages that would follow have been mentioned. They are enormous. But even assuming that Polsby and Wildavsky are too pessimistic, that the two parties would survive, and that the work of making a coalition would proceed in each party between the first primary and the runoff, the upshot would be a coalition-forming procedure scarcely more responsive to an appropriate constituency than the most irresponsible convention we are likely to witness. The two top contenders would have been chosen by popular pluralities, to be sure, though their vote is likely to be of the order of 20 to 25 per cent, and whatever choice between them the rest of the candidates and their manager made would require ratification in the runoff, just as convention choices are up for ratification in the election now. But, subject to this constraint, which operates equally on the conventions, the candidates and the managers would make their decision in some back room, at least as free of any other constraint as the convention bosses who picked Harding in 1920. This is scarcely what the proponents of the national primary intend, yet it is what they would get—at best.

Selection of Convention Delegates

To reject the national primary is not to concede, however, that the national party convention as we now know it is acceptable. No American political institution is more visible than the convention, or more often visibly shoddy, and none is less visibly constituted and managed. An examination of the 1968 Democratic Convention, for example, reveals some rather remarkable practices, which are common, with an occasional variation, in the Republican Party as well.

There are states where all or part of the delegation to the national convention is appointed by the governor or state chairman (e.g., Georgia, Louisiana); or by the state executive committee (e.g., New York), which may last have been elected two or four years earlier (e.g., Pennsylvania, Maryland); or by a state convention whose members, in turn, are appointed by local party functionaries (e.g., Michigan, Illinois). The Democratic Convention was studied in the summer of 1968 by an unofficial, privately funded Commission on the Democratic Selection of Presidential Nominees, of which Governor, now Senator, Harold E. Hughes of Iowa was chairman. (It was brought together on the initiative of a few delegates who were members of the Convention's Credentials and Rules Committees, and it made recommendations and issued a report from which the facts about the convention that I am here able to recite are chiefly drawn.[2]) Over 600 delegates to the 1968 Convention, the Hughes Commission found—approximately half the number needed to win a nomination—"were selected by processes which have included no means [however indirect] of voter participation since 1966." This is utterly unjustifiable.

A party's professional cadre should, no doubt, have a voice. The professionals are, if nothing else, a faction that deserves representation, and it is sound institutional policy to reward their services with a measure of influence. They symbolize, moreover, the continuity of the party, and play a principal role in giving it an identity. Their greatest interest is the party's own institutional interest in winning—at least as it is vouchsafed to them to see that interest over the long term. But if they lend the party its character of an "organized appetite," as

---

[2] In addition to Senator Hughes, the Commission consisted of Representative Donald M. Fraser of Minnesota, who served as vice-chairman, Harry Ashmore, Julian Bond, Frederick G. Dutton, Mrs. Doris Fleeson Kimball, and the present writer. Its staff was headed by Thomas P. Alder as director, Geoffrey Cowan as associate director, and Simon Lazarus as editor. The Commission's report is entitled *The Democratic Choice*. See also Paul T. David, Ralph M. Goldman, and Richard C. Bain, *The Politics of National Party Conventions* (Washington, D.C.: The Brookings Institution, 1960), pp. 249ff.

Felix Frankfurter once wrote,[3] their appetite is sometimes keener for power in the organization than for organizing to secure the power of government. At any rate, no one need fear that the professionals will go unrepresented. Even in states where delegates are elected in direct primaries, the cadre knows how to maintain its foothold, as David, Goldman, and Bain have pointed out.[4] The problem in constructing a convention is not to assure a voice for the professionals, but to dislodge them from a controlling position.

Methods of delegate selection that do bear scrutiny, as appointment by the professional cadre will not, are election by a state convention to which representatives are chosen, in turn, either directly or through an additional stage of district conventions, at precinct caucuses open to all party members; and direct election either in a winner-take-all, at-large primary as in California, or in at-large and district primaries, with (e.g., New Hampshire) or without (e.g., New Jersey) an accompanying statewide preferential poll, in which the people have a chance to vote for actual Presidential candidates.

It would be difficult and unwise to opt on a national basis for any one of these acceptable methods to the exclusion of the other ones. The winner-take-all state primary has its virtues. It is a trial heat, a shakedown cruise for candidates, and a preview for the public. It catches attention and generates interest. Politics is an educational endeavor before and after it is anything else, and in this endeavor the major state primary helps. The drama is heightened for all concerned by the winner-take-all feature; for the candidate with little support from the professionals, the attractiveness of the primary is enhanced, as for the public is its authenticity as a preview. And the winner-take-all primary injects into the convention's

[3] Felix Frankfurter, *Law and Politics* (New York: Capricorn Books, 1962), p. 316.
[4] *The Politics of National Party Conventions*, p. 243.

process of judgment a prediction that is more than a guess, and more reliable than a poll, of what the party faces in the general election. But the statewide, winner-take-all primary as universal practice would avoid few of the shortcomings of a national primary. If a reasonably obvious national winner was turned up, the convention would be supposed merely to register the choice. Or else, if as would more often happen the state primaries produced no conclusive winner, the convention's task would be what it is today, but its composition would be most unsuited to a satisfactory performance of that task.

There are by and large, as I have been implying, two sorts of multi-member democratic institutions: the representative, deliberative assembly, and the body meant to register a single prior decision of its constituency. Congress is the typical institution of the former sort, the electoral college of the latter. (He did not "choose Samuel Miles to determine for me whether John Adams or Thomas Jefferson is the fittest man for President of the United States," said a Federalist voter of a member of the electoral college in 1796. "No, I choose him to act, not to think.") Institutions meant to act by registering the decision of a majority of their constituency should consist of members responsive to that majority, and of no one else. Deliberative institutions, charged also to think, should reflect as many significant factions in the total constituency as possible. That is why all American legislatures are districted. None is elected at large, to be a creature wholly of the majority, nor does any state send to Congress an entire delegation elected on a statewide basis. It is particularly necessary to represent the minority in a deliberative assembly that sits briefly and only periodically, and has as its sole object the composition of a governing coalition. The minority must be there, quite simply, in order that some portion of it may be coalesced with; or to put it in other terms, no relevant majority exists for purposes of constituting such a deliberative assembly until the assembly's own majority-building work is done, and that work can be done only if the total or near-total constituency is present through its delegates.

The only thing that might be said for a convention consisting entirely of members chosen in winner-take-all primaries would be that as a registering sort of institution it would, like the electoral college, be weighted in favor of the large states. But the justification for such a double weighting is not easily found. It certainly cannot be the same justification as that which supports using the electoral college to choose a President who will function jointly with a Congress oriented toward a different constituency, especially since the fact that in the general election the college gives the large states a disproportionate voice is itself a consideration affecting the judgment of any convention, whatever its composition. In any case, the short answer is that the convention must be a deliberative, not a registering institution. And so delegations chosen in winner-take-all primaries, speaking for a majority or perhaps a plurality of a state party, are welcome as one element in the mix of the convention, not as the universal element.

Delegations selected in district primaries are likely, subject to the accidents of geography, to represent minorities as well as majorities in a state party, and so are delegations chosen at state conventions whose members were elected at open precinct caucuses—but this last will be so only if one highly important condition has been met. At many precinct caucuses, district conventions, and then state conventions, the unit rule prevails, so that at each stage minorities may be left unrepresented, because majorities at precinct caucuses or at district conventions may pick all the delegates to the state convention without minority representation, and the state convention can then also pick the delegation to the national convention by majority vote without minority representation. This is, to be sure, not the practice everywhere, but the Hughes Commission confirmed some of Senator McCarthy's complaints that it was the practice used to his disadvantage by the Democratic Party in some states; and used here and there, one may add, by the McCarthy people themselves, when they had the chance. Where as an act of grace some representation is given to the minority, it is often not in due proportion to its strength.

The result is the same as in winner-take-all primaries, except that a winner-take-all precinct caucus and convention system has none of the virtues of the popular primary. Hence, while accepting the value of the winner-take-all primary in a few states, the Hughes Commission recommended absolute abolition of the unit rule at all levels, abolition as well, of course, of any system of "direct appointment" of delegations, in whole or in part, by state party executives or other officials; and the selection of delegates by procedures that "permit meaningful popular participation" within a period of not more than "six months before the Convention itself."

Somewhat to everyone else's surprise, and perhaps also to its own, the 1968 Democratic Convention adopted the following resolution offered by a minority of its Rules Committee:

> It is understood that a state Democratic Party, in selecting and certifying delegates to the National Convention, thereby undertakes to assure that such delegates have been selected through a process in which all Democratic voters have had full and timely opportunity to participate. In determining whether a state party has complied with this mandate, the convention shall require that:
>
> (1) The unit rule not be used in any stage of the delegate selection process; and

(2) All feasible efforts have been made to assure that delegates are selected through party primary, convention, or committee procedures open to public participation within the calendar year of the National Convention.

This is almost the whole of the Hughes Commission recommendation. In addition, as the Hughes Commission also suggested, the chairman of the Democratic National Committee was instructed to set up a special committee charged with helping the states implement these policies.

The millennium is not yet here. The language of the resolution is in some respects fairly specific—no unit rule; party primary, convention, or committee procedures open to the public "within the calendar year"—and means that most professional appointment and minority-exclusion practices (in nonprimary states) are out. But appointment of some delegates, as in New York, by a state committee, itself elected in the year of the convention, remains possible. Even where it is specific and entirely satisfactory, moreover, the policy must be implemented, and there are portions of it which are not all that specific and which call for further legislative efforts prior to implementation. Thus "procedures open to public participation" is a phrase that can do with a lot of explaining.

Racial Discrimination and Exclusion

The general contours of the course of legislation and implementation that has to follow may be foretold from the experience with an earlier attempt at reform in the Democratic Party. At the 1964 Democratic Convention in Atlantic City, an all-white Mississippi delegation was challenged not merely on the obvious ground that Negroes were unrepresented even though Mississippi has a considerable Negro population, but on the basis also of extensive proofs that by concerted and

deliberate action the Mississippi Democratic Party had excluded Negroes from its affairs. Negroes were often effectively deterred from attending precinct meetings by threats of
economic and physical harm. Information of the times and
places of meetings was withheld from them, and if they
somehow did show up, they were denied parliamentary rights.
Moreover, the Mississippi Democratic Party openly pro-
claimed racist principles, as did also the Republicans in Mississippi. In 1964, both the Democratic and Republican state
platforms endorsed segregation. Since the Mississippi election
law provides that "no person shall be eligible to participate in
any primary election unless he . . . is in accord" with the
state platform of the party in whose primary he wishes to vote,
Negroes were quite plainly invited out of both the Democratic and the Republican parties. The absence of any Negro
on the Mississippi delegation to the 1964 Democratic Convention merely dramatized these grievances.

With the mediating assistance of the then Senator Hubert
Humphrey, the 1964 Convention adjudicated the Mississippi
challenge retroactively by reaching a compromise, and pros-
pectively by adopting a strong statement of principle. Two
Mississippi Negroes were seated as delegates-at-large, and the
all-white regular delegation was also seated. But for the
future, Mississippi and all other states were required to afford
to all voters, regardless of race, "the opportunity to participate
fully in party affairs." Mere contrived representation of Negroes on state delegations would not do in the future. That
much was in effect ordered retroactively in 1964 as well. The
decision did not—as would the 1968 resolution—prescribe
democratic methods of delegate selection. It did not, indeed,
have specific reference to the process of delegate selection,
and certainly not exclusive reference to it. It meant that, as a
condition to being seated in 1968, state parties had to give
free and full opportunity to Negroes to participate at all levels

of party activity, at all times, whatever the method might ultimately be by which delegates were selected, and whatever sort of delegation that method ultimately produced.

This, if with a little bit of backing and filling, was the understanding of a Special Equal Rights Committee set up by the Democratic National Committee to implement the 1964 decision. A report of the Special Committee in April, 1966, still found vestiges of discrimination, and put the state parties on notice that none would be seated in 1968 which failed to change "rules, laws, and procedures" tending "to bar full Party participation." There was no suggestion that the inclusion of some token Negroes on a delegation could purchase legitimacy from the national Democratic Party in 1968. Nor was there any such suggestion in a letter of July, 1967, to all state party chairmen from a new chairman of the Special Equal Rights Committee, Governor Richard Hughes of New Jersey. This letter set forth "minimal prerequisites" for any program of implementing the decision of the 1964 Convention. All public meetings, at all levels, it said, must be open to party members regardless of race. And the times and places of public meetings at all levels and the procedures for selection of party officers must be fully publicized.

Any narrower understanding of the intent and coverage of the 1964 decision, limiting it somehow to the delegate-selection process rather than viewing it as applicable to party affairs in general, on all levels, at all times, hardly seemed possible. For in most states, prior to the sort of reform set in train at the 1968 Convention, no easy distinction can be taken between party affairs in general and those directly related to the delegate-selection process. Party officials influence the choice of delegates, to say the least, and it is not altogether unusual, as we have seen, for state committees to select delegates directly, without submitting their choices to anyone's ratification. Hence meaningful participation in the choice of the state's delegation to the national convention has to be participation at a much earlier stage of party affairs. A 1968 report of the United States Civil Rights Commission quotes a South Carolina NAACP official as saying: "If you don't get in at the precinct meeting, you are out."[5]

The 1968 Convention, at which Governor Richard Hughes of New Jersey (who had headed the Special Equal Rights Committee of the Democratic National Committee) was chairman of the convention's Credentials Committee, seeing that nothing had changed in Mississippi since 1964, excluded the regular Mississippi delegation. In a compromise action, it also unseated half of the regular Georgia delegation. But the United States Civil Rights Commission's 1968 report, based on investigations of the 1966 and 1967 elections in Southern states, found substantial evidence of several kinds of discriminatory action against Negroes in party affairs also in Alabama and South Carolina. In Barbour and Montgomery counties, Alabama, measures were taken to prevent election of Negroes to the Democratic county executive committees, and in Choctaw County, Alabama, to prevent their serving as election officials. In Dallas County, Alabama, of which Selma of 1965 fame is the seat, the Democratic county executive committee is self-perpetuating, the members filling vacancies. This is a system which, of course, locks in all past discriminations against Negroes. It has precisely the vice of requirements, long since declared unconstitutional by the federal courts, that any new voter be vouched for by an old one. The effect in places where no, or very few, Negroes voted in the past is obvious. In South Carolina, the Civil Rights Commission found evidence that Negroes were excluded from some precinct meetings in Dorchester and Williamsburg counties. And in Alabama as well as Georgia, state party officials declared to Commission interviewers that they were powerless to

[5] United States Commission on Civil Rights, *Political Participation* (Washington, D.C., 1968), p. 60.

deal with discrimination within the Democratic Party at the county level.[6]

Conceivably these abuses in Alabama and South Carolina were remedied to the satisfaction of the Credentials Committee of the 1968 Convention. More probably, they were considered relatively minor, and were overlooked. The Alabama and South Carolina delegations were in any event seated. The Harold Hughes Commission on the Democratic Selection of Presidential Nominees urged the convention to adopt a recommendation of the United States Civil Rights Commission spelling out in great detail, and with an eye to practices of racial exclusion actually in use, the nondiscrimination policy that state parties should be required to implement. (See Appendix IX.) But the convention did not take up this recommendation. The Hughes Commission also suggested that in the future, when a challenge to a delegation is based on credible evidence of racial discrimination—such as a showing of one or more instances of exclusion based on race at any level of party activity, or a showing that the representation of Negroes on the delegation is grossly disproportionate to the percentage of Negroes in the population of the state—the burden of proof before the Credentials Committee of the convention should shift from the challenger to the challenged delegation. An analogous shift in the burden of proof is a technique central to the enforcement machinery provided in the Voting Rights Act of 1965. Under Section 4(a) of that act, a state or county wishing to reinstitute a literacy test for voting, for example, which was suspended by the act, must come into federal court and prove that for a period of five years no such test has been used for the purpose, or with the effect, of discriminating against Negro voters. But the Hughes Commission recommendation for shifting the burden of proof was also ignored by the 1968 Convention.

One draws the conclusion that the 1964 nondiscrimination

[6] *Ibid.*, pp. 23–24, 61–64, 102–104, 134, 138–139.

policy has been implemented by the national Democratic Party, but in a spirit of gradualism. And one surmises that a certain gradualism is likely to characterize implementation of the new policy adopted in 1968 as well. The Republican Party, on the other hand, has not even reached the threshold of gradualism, either on the racial problem, or on the question of delegate-selection methods in general.

Access to the Party

In the course of implementation of the 1968 Democratic Convention's resolution on methods of delegate selection, a difficult problem, not yet considered, is bound to surface. It concerns access to the party and adherence to it or, if you will, the definition of the party. One aspect of this problem emerged in the loyalty oath controversies that have bedeviled the Democratic Party for a generation.

The American major party is a coalition formed every four years from a center of gravity that is apt to shift every so often. The stable factor—although this is not always true either, witness the dance around each other's flanks executed by the Democrats and Republicans in the William Jennings Bryan–Alton B. Parker–Theodore Roosevelt–Wilson years— is that the center of gravity of the Republicans is somewhere to the right of the Democratic one and, at any rate, always somewhat different. But each party reaches out every four years, the one usually to the left, the other usually to the right, and both toward the center of the continuum of public opinion and private interest, in the effort to create as large a governing majority as its centripetal force can command. Therefore, although each has a professional cadre, and although each exerts its centripetal force from a different point on the spectrum of opinion and interest, each is also something of a new coalition every quadrennium.

The implications for the loyalty oath issue, which the Democrats ultimately accepted, are that it is hardly consistent to require any group, as a condition for coming to the convention and engaging in the coalition-making process, to promise beforehand to abide by the result, even though, as may happen, it is affirmatively excluded from the coalition. The convention is the occasion of forming the party for a particular election, and no one can say with detailed assurance beforehand what kind of a party it will be. Hence, although the issue was fudged somewhat in the patchwork compromise about the Georgia delegation at the 1968 Democratic Convention, the Democrats require only that delegates promise to use their influence to see to it that the nominees of the convention are listed as Democratic nominees on the ballot in their states, not that they promise necessarily to support the nominees.

The implications for procedures of delegate selection should be similar. It ought not to be necessary, as in many states it is, to have been a registered Democrat or Republican at some prior time in order to participate in a Democratic or Republican primary, or in party caucuses. The party ought each year to be open to all those groups which in that year wish to enter into the process of forming the coalition that will be the Democratic or Republican Party. If the parties were as open as they should be, large numbers of people who had voted Democratic in the past might in 1968 have moved to form in the Republican Party a coalition around Rockefeller, or Charles Percy, or John Lindsay, oriented more to the right than would normally suit them, but more satisfactory to them in that year than what they foresaw as the Democratic combination. Or else anti-Vietnam Republicans might have helped put together in the Democratic Party an alliance turning on the war issue, under such a candidate as Eugene

McCarthy. But the truly open party would encounter difficulties, more serious in primaries than in local caucuses and conventions, and more serious in precinct caucuses than in state, let alone national, conventions, with their larger membership, more demanding activities, and greater exposure.

The trouble is that each party is periodically a new coalition, all right, but each is also, and ought to be, an organism with a continuous existence, particular characteristics, and a corps of permanently loyal supporters. And the two parties must compete, else there will soon be one, and then many, whether in the guise of parties or factions. What can happen when the permanent loyalists are free to float is exemplified in the few states that do allow crossover of voters, or that might allow, as California did until just recently, cross-filing by candidates. The upshot in California in primaries for state office was the nomination, not infrequently, of the same man in both primaries. This destroyed party competition rather effectively. Nor is competition apt to flourish when there is a crossover of voters intent on selecting the candidate most desirable from the other party's point of view, the weakest candidate, easiest to beat. The crossover voter may also be happy with the probable (or certain, if there is no contest) outcome in his own party, and go into the other primary in search of, as nearly as possible, the same result. This is not coalition-building, but coalition-duplicating. It is too nearly the same as the joint nomination of a single man through cross-filing. The two parties would not discharge their function if they did not overlap, or if they assumed polar positions, but though the ground on which they maneuver for differentiation is narrow, they must remain distinct in order to remain two. Party caucuses open to everyone are also subject to being captured by forces wishing to short-circuit party competition.

Nothing in the resolution adopted at the 1968 Democratic Convention suggests a way out of this dilemma. The special committee to be established by the Democratic National

Committee will need to grapple with it on its own. In the Republican Party, any approach to a solution of this problem, as to other reforms, is even more remote. The Democratic Committee will probably be inclined at first to go along with restrictive practices, which grant access to the party only to those who have in the past indicated adherence to it, or at least not registered as members of the other party. That would be understandable, but wrong. The open party, with its risks, is the prime objective. For party habits are strong, and Machiavellian crossovers, while they occur, are rare. What is more common, and should be encouraged, is unaffiliated floating by voters who, if excluded at the nominating stage, are likely to be disaffected by the limitations of choice in the general election.

Each party should, accordingly, be open in each election year, in primaries and caucuses, to everyone willing at that time to register as a member. The registration would be largely symbolic and would not necessarily exclude crossovers, if for no other reason than that it would be as impossible as it would be ill-advised to try to bind individuals to vote the party ticket in the general election. But the symbolism would be endowed with some consequences. Certainly it should be provided that a voter may participate in the nominating process of only one major party in any given year.

Apportionment of Voting Power
in the Convention

Delegate-selection methods are not the only feature of the convention that leaves something to be desired. Another is the complicated formula for apportioning voting power among the states. It begins in both parties—and has done so since conventions came into being in 1832—with the electoral college scheme. In the 1968 Democratic Convention, for example, states received three votes for each vote they have in the electoral college. In addition, every state has two votes on the Democratic National Committee, and it got a convention vote for each of these. (See Appendix X.) The next step in both parties is a bonus system, as it is called. In the 1968 Democratic Convention, one bonus vote was awarded for each 100,000 popular votes cast in a state for the Democratic nominees at the last Presidential election, and on top of that there was a ten-vote bonus if the Democratic nominees carried the state. (See Appendix X.) The end result is a considerable, if helter-skelter, departure from the population standard of representation. It is not that all the larger states are handicapped, although many of them were in 1968, or that any single region is favored or disfavored, although that will happen if the last previous ticket had some marked regional strengths or weaknesses, as the Republican ticket did in 1964; it is just that from the point of view of representing population there is considerable disarray.

The peculiar purpose that the electoral college system serves in the general election could be fulfilled in the convention only if all delegations were chosen in winner-take-all popular primaries, and happily—as noted earlier—they are not. So this purpose is simply irrelevant to the convention. There is a certain fitness, and little harm in a body so large, in following the electoral college scheme to the extent of giving the smaller states something of an advantage; the composition of the Senate does so in Congress. There is no justification, however, for giving them an additional bonus, as if they were to have four Senators, by letting them vote their two representatives on the Democratic National Committee also. Again, a flat ten-vote reward for carrying the state for the Democratic nominee—the same whether for New York or Montana—is a further unjustified weighting of representation in favor of the smaller states, especially since quite properly there is a proportional bonus for having attracted more popular support, namely, one convention vote for each 100,000 popular votes cast for the ticket. The Hughes Commission recommended elimination of the extra votes for the Democratic National Committee membership and of the flat ten-vote bonus. But these recommendations were ignored at the 1968 Convention.

Convention Management and Floor Proceedings

The Hughes Commission had some suggestions also concerning the management of the convention and proceedings on the floor. One of these, which called for abolition of the unit rule in casting the vote of any delegation, was adopted by the 1968 Democratic Convention. It was about time. The unit rule never became entrenched in Republican conventions. As long ago as 1880, the Republicans repudiated it with complete finality.

Other Hughes Commission recommendations were not accepted by the 1968 Convention, and among them were these: that voting within the Democratic National Committee, which exercises vast powers in planning and controlling the convention, be weighted in proportion to the convention votes of each state; that chairmen of convention committees, such as Rules, Platform, and Credentials, be appointed well in advance of the convention and be provided with adequate staff; that the votes of members of these committees, in which the coalition-building process really begins in earnest, and on which the states are now equally represented, be weighted in proportion to each state's voting power in the convention itself; that if a challenge to a delegation is supported by at least a 10 per cent minority of the Credentials Committee, that delegation not be permitted to vote on any question before the convention until the challenge has been resolved, barring only the case where an opening would thus be given for an attempt to pack the convention, as when challenges are directed at a number of delegations which together comprise more than 20 per cent of the total voting power at the convention; that the party pay a per diem expense allowance to delegates, so that persons of moderate means may find it more nearly possible to accept service as members of the convention; and that a roll-call vote be obtainable not only, as at present, at the request of eight delegations, but also at the request of 20 per cent of the delegates, so that a roll call can be forced by a minority that is dispersed geographically, as well as by minorities that are concentrated regionally.

Each of these recommendations, rejected by the Democrats, is aimed at correcting practices that prevail in closely similar form in the Republican Party, too, although in the Eisenhower-Taft contest at the 1952 Republican Convention, delegations under a challenge supported by more than one third of the Credentials Committee were not permitted to vote at all before final resolution of the challenge on the convention floor. Another serious flaw is the elephantiasis of the conventions, and it is greatly and increasingly more serious in the Democratic than in the Republican Party. There were 2,477 delegates to the 1956 Democratic Convention, casting 1,372 votes, many of them, obviously, fractional. The Republicans had 1,323 delegates, all of them entitled to a full vote. That is still a great many, but the size of the Republican Convention has remained fairly stable. The Democrats in 1968 nearly doubled the number of votes—to a total of 2,622—in an effort to eliminate fractional voting. The end result was an increase not only in votes but in membership. There are, in addition, alternates, who at the 1968 Democratic Convention numbered almost again as many—2,512. (See Appendix X.)

No parliamentary body can operate effectively as a parliament—it can operate as something else, but not as what it ought to be—even at the size of the Republican Convention, let alone at the preposterous one the Democrats have let themselves arrive at. The idea initially, in the 1830's, was of a body more or less the size of Congress. As things are now, David, Goldman, and Bain have justly charged, both individual delegations and the convention as a whole "provide apt illustration" of Madison's remark in the 58th *Federalist* "that in all legislative assemblies the greater the number composing them may be, the fewer will be the men who will in fact direct their proceedings."[7] And assuredly the general atmosphere of the convention—about which the less said, the better—and the inconsequence of much that goes on at it are in some part functions of undue size.

The issues touched on in this section, as well as those dealt with earlier, some of which are, to be sure, more basic, will have to be addressed honestly and intelligently—and soon—if the inadequately representative, at once disorderly and over-controlled convention that we now have is to become the responsible and respected deliberative institution it must be.

[7] *The Politics of National Party Conventions*, p. 215.

4

Minor Parties

THE SURVIVAL of the convention and of the two-party system it sustains is not a unanimously shared objective, particularly in this season. Its virtues rather than its imperfections gain for the two-party system its most implacable enemies. The moderate coalition, the sensible accommodation, the muted ideology, the politicians who strive to borrow each other's protective coloration and who jostle one another in the center—all this, the price of broadly based government, of general acquiescence, and of stability, is paid in frustration. The choice in the general election between two candidates either of whom can satisfy most people, or at least radically dissatisfy very few, always leaves some of us with no choice at all. Hence the minor party, a steady obbligato in our political symphony. It is sometimes a regional, and commonly an ideological, interest group, which has not been accommodated because it wants something too precise, too clear-cut, because it wants it on principle now and not later, wants all of it, wants it intensely, of course, and wants it when someone who is otherwise in a better position to bargain wants the very opposite with equal intensity.

The minor party is also a group which has summoned the courage to bring prematurely to the fore a basic issue, perhaps a moral one, that the country must face, and in time will face. The word "prematurely" is used here from the point of view of the major parties, the defect of whose virtues is that they are liable to be sluggish in addressing newly arisen fundamental issues, moral ones especially. They are too intent on power to take the risk before they have to. Again and again, minor parties have led from a flank, while the major parties still followed opinion down the middle. In time, the middle has moved, and one of the major parties or both occupy the ground reconnoitered by the minor party; or to change the figure, the major parties, as Disraeli said of Peel and the Whigs, at last catch the minor parties bathing and walk away with their clothes. So it was with the antislavery Free Soilers, with the Populists in 1892, with the LaFollette Progressives, and even the earlier Eugene V. Debs Socialists—and, to be sure, with the Prohibitionists, who are a useful reminder that the Anti-Masonic, Know-Nothing, Thurmond States' Rights, and George Wallace Independent parties must not go unmentioned, lest small-party romanticism run away with one. But as an outlet for frustration, as often a creative force and a sort of conscience, as an ideological governor to keep major parties from speeding off into an abyss of mindlessness, and even just as a technique for strengthening a group's bargaining position for the future, the minor party would have to be invented if it did not come into existence regularly enough. It is an indispensable part of the system whose beneficent chief aim is to suppress it. And its existence is at any rate constitutionally protected.

The Constitutional Position

The two-party system, as the late Justice Robert H. Jackson once said in another context, is a political practice "which has its origin in custom [and] must rely upon custom for its sanctions."[1] Even though, therefore, it is up to state legislatures under Article II, Section 1 of the Constitution to prescribe the manner in which electors who will choose a

---

[1] *Ray* v. *Blair,* 343 U.S. 214, 233 (1952) (Jackson, J., dissenting).

President and Vice-President are themselves to be chosen, an attempt by law to secure the major parties' monopoly of Presidential power would most assuredly fail. It would founder against the Equal Protection Clause of the Fourteenth Amendment, which forbids unreasonable discrimination among voters and also among candidates; which, in other words, safeguards a right to vote free from unreasonable discriminations, and also a right to be a candidate. And it would run afoul as well of the First Amendment, as incorporated into the Due Process Clause of the Fourteenth, for the First Amendment has been interpreted to guarantee a right of effective political association, and that right would be denied by any statute making it impossible to achieve the end for which political association is ultimately undertaken.

A decade ago, a suit to gain a place on the ballot for a minor party or an independent candidate might have failed at the outset for jurisdictional reasons. Federal courts were loath to exercise supervision over the electoral process, although even then they readily intervened under the Fifteenth Amendment, which guarantees freedom from racial discrimination in the exercise of the franchise, so that, for example, they invalidated a registration period which they found to be too short and thus too onerous an obstacle to Negro registration.[2] But the jurisdictional barrier, such as it was, was conclusively removed by *Baker* v. *Carr*,[3] the first of the reapportionment cases—which, whatever one may think of its progeny and of the doctrine of one man, one vote as it later evolved, did render the law more rational and self-consistent on the jurisdictional issue.

No state actually decrees in so many words that in order to be allowed to vote or run for President or for Presidential elector, a person must be a member, or submit himself to the

[2] See *Lane* v. *Wilson*, 307 U.S. 268 (1939).
[3] 369 U.S. 186 (1962).

procedures, of the Democratic or Republican Party. And only Ohio has come near to saying as much indirectly. Ohio has allowed no independent, nonparty candidacy; and a minor party could place a candidate on the ballot only if it filed a petition signed by voters equal in number to 15 per cent of the total vote cast in the last gubernatorial election—in 1968, upwards of 430,000. Additional difficulties were also put in the way. The minor party had to organize itself through primary elections on the same scale as the major ones, and persons who voted in a major party primary at the previous election were not qualified to participate in organizing the minor party. On October 15, 1968, in the first decision of its kind, the Supreme Court held the Ohio scheme unconstitutional. The suit was brought in behalf of George Wallace, whose name the Court ordered placed on the ballot. The Ohio election law, said the opinion of the Court, delivered by Justice Black, had a "crippling impact" on "basic constitutional rights." It imposed "a burden on voting and associational rights which we hold is an invidious discrimination. . . ."[4] A federal district judge had remarked at an earlier stage of the case that the " 'two-party system' is not a cliché in Ohio, but a statutorily enforced fact."[5] It is no more.

Other states may not quite make the two-party monopoly a statutory fact, but a great many make life hard for the minor party. The requirement of signatures on a petition in a number equal to 15 per cent of the total vote at a past election, itself a grave impediment, is rare, but Arkansas imposes it also. And a number of states have distribution requirements, which also present serious obstacles. Thus in Idaho a

---

[4] *Williams v. Rhodes,* Nos. 543 and 544, O.T. 1968, Supreme Court of the United States, October 15, 1968.
[5] *Williams v. Rhodes,* Civil Action Nos. 68–244, 68–248, United States District Court for the Southern District of Ohio, Eastern Division, August 29, 1968 (Kinneary, J., dissenting).

petition must be signed by 3,000 voters, no more than 150 of whom are residents of any single county; Illinois requires 25,000 signatures, with 200 from each of at least 50 counties; and New York requires 12,000, 50 at least from each county. In Florida, where a very substantial portion of the population is in Dade County, no more than 13.3 per cent of the total number of necessary signatures may come from any single county, and a small percentage must come from each of 34 counties. Finally, a great many states, while they have workable provisions for getting a new ticket on the ballot, set a very early date for qualification, as early as March in Pennsylvania and Alabama, April in Kentucky and West Virginia, May in Michigan and New Jersey, and June, July, and August in many more.

The legal question concerning conditions of the sort just described is, how difficult may a state make it for anyone but the Democratic or Republican nominee to get on the ballot? It is generally held in voting cases under the Fourteenth and Fifteenth Amendments, and in free speech and association cases under the First, that what the state may not absolutely forbid, prevent, or punish, it may also not render onerous, except for the most exigent of reasons. Thus when Oklahoma prescribed a very short time in which Negroes could register, making registration difficult for them, the Court held that the Fifteenth Amendment had been violated. There was no need for the Negro plaintiffs to try to show that Oklahoma had absolutely prevented their registration.[6] And the poll tax was declared unconstitutional under the Fourteenth Amendment without a showing that it utterly deprived people of the franchise; it was enough that the tax placed a burden on the right to vote.[7] Similarly in First Amendment cases, it was not

[6] *Lane* v. *Wilson, supra.* See also *Louisiana* v. *United States,* 380 U.S. 145 (1965); *United States* v. *Mississippi,* 380 U.S. 128 (1965).
[7] *Harper* v. *Virginia Board of Elections,* 383 U.S. 663 (1966).

necessary to prove that membership in the NAACP, for example, or in other organizations, had been altogether forbidden; it was enough of a First Amendment violation that membership had been made difficult, risky.[8]

A court could be urged to hold, therefore, that since a state may not forbid minor parties, it may also not discriminate against them. Any discrimination against minor parties and in favor of the two established ones, the argument would run, whether "crippling" like the Ohio scheme, or just inconvenient, is unconstitutional. But it would be wrong to press matters that far. The states are entitled to put some store by the two-party system, and they ought to have the power to give it a certain edge. Yet it is a long way from achievement of this objective to choking off all political action that is not encompassed by the two major parties; this the states may not do, and the problem is to define what amounts to doing it. In general terms, the courts would probably agree to the proposition that laws which make it impossible for an initially small group of voters to put a candidate on the ballot through a reasonable and not prohibitively expensive effort in a reasonable amount of time are unconstitutional. A criterion such as this should work out to render unconstitutional a requirement for obtaining the signatures of anything over 5 per cent of the electorate. Most states are in fact satisfied with a good deal less.

Under existing analogous judicial decisions, the most vulnerable requirements are those concerning distribution. The Illinois one was upheld by the Supreme Court in 1948,[9] but

[8] See, e.g., *NAACP v. Alabama,* 357 U.S. 449 (1958); *Bates v. Little Rock,* 361 U.S. 516 (1960); *NAACP v. Flowers,* 377 U.S. 288 (1964); *Gibson v. Florida Investigation Committee,* 372 U.S. 539 (1963); *DeGregory v. Attorney General,* 383 U.S. 825 (1966).
[9] *MacDougall v. Green,* 335 U.S. 281 (1948); see also *Moore v. Shapiro,* Civil Action No. 68C1569, United States District Court for the Northern District of Illinois, Eastern Division, October 3, 1968.

that was before the Supreme Court's more recent reapportionment decisions. Today it could be strongly argued that any
distribution requirement is a form of malapportionment, a
way of giving more weight to a signature in a small county
than in a large one, and therefore invalid under the reapportionment cases. It is invalid, one may say in passing, for better
reasons than malapportionment of a legislature itself. Malapportionment of a deliberative body may serve the purpose of
representing all of a state's varied interest groups in it. This
consideration is hardly relevant to standards for allowing a
Presidential or other statewide candidate to appear on the
ballot. Moreover, the power of a malapportioned legislature is
balanced by that of a governor, whose constituency operates
strictly on the majoritarian principle.

Qualifying Dates

Early qualifying dates obviously do not in themselves present insuperable barriers. The argument against many of
them would be that a state may seek to foster the two-party
system, and to this end discriminate against independent
candidates, but—administrative and housekeeping necessities
to the side—it may discriminate only by means that are
rationally suited to achieve this end, only by means that in
fact do favor the two-party system.

Now the important third-party movements in our history—
George Wallace in 1968 is a point-proving exception—came
into being after the two major party conventions, and were
enabled to come into being at that time because major party
conventions used to be held much earlier than at present. In
1892, Harrison and Cleveland were nominated in June. The
Populists, disappointed by the Democrats, met later and
nominated a third candidate, General James B. Weaver. In
1912, Theodore Roosevelt fought his heart out in the Republican Convention in June. Having been defeated, he formed

the Progressive Party. Again, in 1924, Coolidge and Davis were nominated in June. The third-party LaFollette candidacy took shape in July.

The characteristic American third party, then, consists of a group of people who have tried to exert influence within one of the major parties, have failed, and later decide to work on the outside. States in which there is an early qualifying date tend to force such groups to create minor parties without first attempting to influence the course taken by a major one. For a dissident group is put to the choice of forgoing major-party primary and other pre-nomination activity by organizing separately early in an election year, or losing all opportunity for action as a third party later. From the point of view of fostering the two-party system this is counterproductive. It is calculated to induce early third-party movements, like the George Wallace party; calculated to drive people away from the coalition-building process that is the genius of the two-party system, and into a premature and more likely permanent ideological separatism, which is precisely what the two-party system is intended to prevent. One may add that never has it been as evident as this year that unforeseen occurrences in the early portion of an election year can fundamentally affect all political expectations. For administrative reasons, there has to be a cutoff date sometime, but there is more than a little of the capricious in laws that force a commitment to act (within or without the major parties) in at least two states before such an upheaval as President Johnson's withdrawal on March 31, 1968, and in many states before important primaries, not to mention an event like the assassination of Robert F. Kennedy.

Major party conventions now tend to be held in August. Any qualifying date earlier than the end of September can hardly be supported by practical reasons having to do with the printing of ballots and the like. The only purpose of earlier qualifying dates, therefore, can be to encourage two-party action and discourage third parties. This is, to a degree, a valid purpose, but to make people commit themselves to third-party action without trying first to influence the major parties is no way to enhance the two-party system.

It is, of course, not possible to predict in detail just what the courts would do on questions of this kind,[10] but since state election statutes are shot through not only with anti–third party provisions that are wrong on principle, but also with many which positively disserve the objective of protecting the two-party system, wholesale legislative reform is called for, regardless of what the courts may or may not do.

---

[10] A federal court in Alabama held constitutional, by a divided vote, a scheme that in effect amounted to establishing March 1 as the qualification date. (*Hadnott* v. *Amos*, Civil Action No. 2757–N, United States District Court for the Middle District of Alabama, Northern Division, October 11, 1968.) A week later, on October 18, 1968, the Supreme Court summarily reversed the decision. The upshot is not much detailed guidance, but assuredly no encouragement to states with early qualifying dates.

5

Epilogue

THE COUNTRY, Walter Lippmann wrote in September, 1968, "has entered a period of revolutionary change of which no one can foresee the course or the end or the consequences." For, he continued, "the central institutions of the traditional life of man"—the family, the Church, the territorial state, the schools, and the universities—"are increasingly unable to command his allegiance and his obedience." Naturally, Mr. Lippmann's diagnosis was that the old two-party system is shattered. This also is the conclusion of many who speak from positions rather radically to the left of Mr. Lippmann's. For myself, I cannot deny it, but my instinct is to disbelieve it. I thought that such a figure as Robert Kennedy would have been capable even in 1968, let alone four years thence, of restoring a sufficiency of order to what Mr. Lippmann, quoting Erasmus, calls the "irremediable confusion of everything." Men want change, and they turn away, or toward George Wallace, because the major parties are sluggish, but they do not turn in either direction inevitably or irremediably; many of those same people—of both varieties—turned earlier to Robert Kennedy, and many even to Eugene McCarthy.

This is not the place to speculate whether the United States deserves a revolution, needs one, or will get one regardless. But short of a revolution, the work of politics in the United States, and the work of politics even for those who set radical goals, is most effectively and enduringly done within the regime, not in opposition to it as such; within the system whose improvement I advocate, but which I praise. And even if the old two-party system, as Mr. Lippmann says, is shat-

51

tered without knowing it, and destined to come down, it is hardly arguable that for that reason it should hasten to bring itself down with such innovations of at best unpredictable and at worst baneful effect as the direct popular election of Presidents and the national primary. Nor is there any reason why it should not reform its electoral college, its conventions, and its election laws in ways consistent with its nature and designed to advance its values. After all, the system may yet belie the jeremiads and disappoint the revolutionaries. It may persist in the mystery of survival, and against that event, it might as well improve itself.

APPENDIX I

*Electoral College Provisions in the
Constitution of the United States*

ARTICLE II

SECTION 1. The executive Power shall be vested in a President of the United States of America. He shall hold his Office during the Term of four Years, and, together with the Vice-President, chosen for the same Term, be elected, as follows.

Each State shall appoint, in such Manner as the Legislature thereof may direct, a Number of Electors, equal to the whole Number of Senators and Representatives to which the State may be entitled in the Congress: but no Senator or Representative, or Person holding an Office of Trust or Profit under the United States, shall be appointed an Elector.

[The Electors shall meet in their respective States, and vote by Ballot for two persons, of whom one at least shall not be an Inhabitant of the same State with themselves. And they shall make a List of all the Persons voted for, and of the Number of Votes for each; which List they shall sign and certify, and transmit sealed to the Seat of the Government of the United States, directed to the President of the Senate. The President of the Senate shall, in the Presence of the Senate and House of Representatives, open all the Certificates, and the Votes shall then be counted. The Person having the greatest Number of Votes shall be the President, if such Number be a Majority of the whole Number of Electors appointed; and if there be more than one who have such Majority, and have an equal Number of Votes, then the House of Representatives shall immediately chuse by Ballot one of them for President; and if no Person have a Majority, then from the five highest on the List the said House shall in like Manner chuse the President. But in chusing the President, the Votes shall be taken by States, the Representation from each State having one Vote; A quorum for this Purpose shall consist of a Member or Members from two-thirds of the States, and a Majority of all the States shall be necessary to a Choice. In every Case, after the Choice of the President, the Person having the greatest Number of Votes of the Electors shall be the Vice President. But if there should remain two or more who have equal Votes, the Senate shall chuse from them by Ballot the Vice-President.][1]

The Congress may determine the Time of chusing the Electors, and the Day on which they shall give their Votes; which Day shall be the same throughout the United States.

Amendment XII (1804)

The Electors shall meet in their respective states and vote by ballot for President and Vice-President, one of whom, at least, shall not be an inhabitant of the same state with themselves; they shall name in their ballots the person voted for as President, and in distinct ballots the person voted for as Vice-President, and they shall make distinct lists of all persons voted for as President, and of all persons voted for as Vice-President, and of the number of votes for each, which lists they shall sign and certify, and transmit sealed to the seat of the government of the United States, directed to the President of the Senate;—The President of the Senate shall, in presence of the Senate and House of Representatives, open all the certificates and the votes shall then be counted;—The person having the greatest number of votes for President, shall be the President, if such number be a majority of the whole number of Electors appointed; and if no person have such majority, then from the persons having the highest numbers not exceeding three on the list of those voted for as President, the House of Representatives shall choose immediately, by ballot, the President. But in choosing the President, the votes shall be taken by states, the representation from each state having one vote; a quorum for this purpose shall consist of a member or members from two-thirds of

[1] Superseded by the Twelfth Amendment.

the states, and a majority of all the states shall be necessary to a choice. [And if the House of Representatives shall not choose a President whenever the right of choice shall devolve upon them, before the fourth day of March next following, then the Vice-President shall act as President, as in the case of the death or other constitutional disability of the President.—][2] The person having the greatest number of votes as Vice-President, shall be the Vice-President, if such number be a majority of the whole number of Electors appointed, and if no person have a majority, then from the two highest numbers on the list, the Senate shall choose the Vice-President; a quorum for the purpose shall consist of two-thirds of the whole number of Senators, and a majority of the whole number shall be necessary to a choice. But no person constitutionally ineligible to the office of President shall be eligible to that of Vice-President of the United States.

Amendment XX (1933)

Section 1. The terms of the President and Vice President shall end at noon on the 20th day of January, and the terms of Senators and Representatives at noon on the 3d day of January, of the years in which such terms would have ended if this article had not been ratified; and the terms of their successors shall then begin.

Section 2. The Congress shall assemble at least once in every year, and such meeting shall begin at noon on the 3d day of January, unless they shall by law appoint a different day.

Section 3. If, at the time fixed for the beginning of the term of the President, the President elect shall have died, the Vice President elect shall become President. If a President shall not have been chosen before the time fixed for the beginning of his term, or if the President elect shall have failed to qualify, then the Vice President elect shall act as President until a President shall have qualified; and the Congress may by law provide for the case wherein neither a President elect nor a Vice President elect shall have qualified, declaring who shall then act as President, or the

[2] Superseded by Section 3 of the Twentieth Amendment.

manner in which one who is to act shall be selected, and such person shall act accordingly until a President or Vice President shall have qualified.

SECTION 4. The Congress may by law provide for the case of the death of any of the persons from whom the House of Representatives may choose a President whenever the right of choice shall have devolved upon them, and for the case of the death of any of the persons from whom the Senate may choose a Vice President whenever the right of choice shall have devolved upon them.

Amendment XXIII (1961)

SECTION 1. The District constituting the seat of Government of the United States shall appoint in such manner as the Congress may direct:

A number of electors of President and Vice President equal to the whole number of Senators and Representatives in Congress to which the District would be entitled if it were a State, but in no event more than the least populous State; they shall be in addition to those appointed by the States, but they shall be considered, for the purposes of the election of President and Vice President, to be electors appointed by a State; and they shall meet in the District and perform such duties as provided by the twelfth article of amendment.

SECTION 2. The Congress shall have power to enforce this article by appropriate legislation.

APPENDIX II

The American Bar Association Proposal
for the
Direct Popular Election of the President

Two versions of the proposal are printed in this appendix. The first, sponsored by Senator Birch Bayh, Democrat of Indiana, and a number of other Senators, is a somewhat murkier draft than the second, the substitute offered by Senator Everett M. Dirksen, Republican of Illinois. But differences in substance are minor. Perhaps the chief one is that the Dirksen substitute appears to leave it open to Congress to institute a national primary, or otherwise to regulate the nominating process. The Dirksen substitute would also require ratification by special conventions in the states, rather than by legislatures.

[S.J. Res. 2, 90th Cong., first sess.]

JOINT RESOLUTION To amend the Constitution to provide for the direct election of the President and the Vice President of the United States

Resolved by the Senate and House of Representatives of the United States of America in Congress assembled (two-thirds of each House concurring therein), That the following article is proposed as an amendment to the Constitution of the United States, which shall be valid to all intents and purposes as part of the Constitution when ratified by the legislatures of three-fourths of the several States within seven years from the date of its submission by the Congress:

"ARTICLE —

"SECTION 1. At a time determined by the Congress there shall be held in each State and in the District of Columbia an election in which the people thereof shall vote for President and for Vice

President. In such election, each voter shall cast a single ballot for two persons who shall have consented to the joining of their names on the ballot for the offices of President and Vice President.

"The legislature of each State shall prescribe the places and manner of holding such election thereof and shall include on the ballot the names of all pairs of persons who have consented to the joining of their names on the ballot for the offices of President and Vice President but the Congress may at any time by law make or alter such regulations. The voters in each State shall have the qualifications requisite for persons voting therein for Members of the Congress, but nothing in this article shall prohibit a State from adopting a less restrictive residence requirement for voting for President and Vice President than for Members of the Congress, or prohibit the Congress from adopting uniform residence and age requirements for voting in such election.

"The Congress shall prescribe the qualifications for voting and the places and manner of holding such elections in the District of Columbia.

"Within forty-five days after the election, or at such time as the Congress may direct, the official custodian of the election returns of each State and the District of Columbia shall prepare, sign, certify, and transmit sealed to the seat of the Government of the United States, directed to the President of the Senate, a list of all persons for whom votes were cast for President and for Vice President, together with the number of votes cast for each.

"SEC. 2. On the 6th day of January following the election, unless the Congress shall by law appoint a different day not earlier than the 4th day of January and not later than the 10th day of January, the President of the Senate shall, in the presence of the Senate and the House of Representatives, open all the certificates, and the votes shall then be totaled. The persons joined as candidates for President and Vice President, having the greatest number of votes shall be declared elected President and Vice President, respectively, if such number be a plurality amounting to at least 40 per centum of the total number of votes certified. If none of the pairs of persons joined as candidates for President and Vice President shall have at least 40 per centum of the total number of votes certified, then Congress shall provide by law, uniform throughout the United States, for a runoff election to be held between the two pairs of persons joined as candidates for President and Vice President, respectively, who received the highest number of votes certified.

"SEC. 3. If, at the time fixed for the counting of the certified vote totals from the respective States, the presidential candidate who would have been entitled to election as President shall have died, the vice presidential candidate entitled to election as Vice President shall be declared elected President.

"The Congress may by law provide for the case of the death or withdrawal, prior to the election provided for in section 1, of a candidate for President or for Vice President and for the case of the death of both the persons who, except for their death, would have been entitled to become President and Vice President.

"SEC. 4. The Congress shall have power to enforce this article by appropriate legislation."

[S.J. Res. 2, 90th Cong., first sess.]

AMENDMENT

(IN THE NATURE OF A SUBSTITUTE)

Intended to be proposed by Mr. Dirksen to S.J. Res. 2, a joint resolution to provide for the direct election of the President and Vice President of the United States, viz: On page 1 strike out all after the resolving clause and insert in lieu thereof the following:

That the following article is proposed as an amendment to the Constitution of the United States, which shall be valid to all intents and purposes as part of the Constitution when ratified by conventions of three-fourths of the several States within seven years from the date of its submission by the Congress:

"ARTICLE —

"Section 1. The President and Vice President shall be elected by the people of the several States and the district constituting the seat of government of the United States.

"SEC. 2. The electors in each State shall have the qualifications requisite for electors of Senators and Representatives in Congress from that State, except that the legislature of any State may prescribe lesser qualifications with respect to residence and Congress may establish uniform residence and age qualifications.

"SEC. 3. The persons having the greatest number of votes for President and Vice President shall be elected, if such number be at least 40 per centum of the whole number of votes cast for such offices. If no persons have such number, a runoff election shall be held in which the choice of President and Vice President shall be made from the persons who received the two highest numbers of votes for each office.

"SEC. 4. The times, places, and manner of holding such election and entitlement to inclusion on the ballot shall be prescribed in each State by the legislature thereof; but the Congress may at any time by law make or alter such regulations. The Congress shall prescribe by law the time, place, and manner in which the results of such elections shall be ascertained and declared.

"SEC. 5. Each elector shall cast a single vote jointly applicable to President and Vice President. Names of candidates shall not be joined unless they have consented thereto and no candidate shall consent to his name being joined with that of more than one other person.

"SEC. 6. The days for such elections shall be determined by Congress and shall be uniform throughout the United States.

"SEC. 7. The Congress may by law provide for the case of the death of any candidate for President or Vice President before the day on which a President-elect or a Vice-President-elect has been chosen; and for the case of a tie in any election.

"SEC. 8. This article shall be inoperative unless it shall have been ratified as an amendment to the Constitution by conventions of three-fourths of the States within seven years from the date of its submission to the States by the Congress."

APPENDIX III

The Plan for Electing Presidential Electors by Congressional District, Proposed by Senator Karl E. Mundt of South Dakota

[S.J. Res. 12, 90th Cong., first sess.]

JOINT RESOLUTION Proposing an amendment to the Constitution of the United States providing for the election of the President and Vice President

Resolved by the Senate and House of Representatives of the United States of America in Congress assembled (two-thirds of each House concurring therein), That the following article is proposed as an amendment to the Constitution of the United States which shall be valid to all intents and purposes as part of the Constitution if ratified by the legislatures of three-fourths of the several States within seven years from the date of its submission by the Congress:

"ARTICLE —

"SECTION 1. Each State shall choose a number of electors of President and Vice President equal to the whole number of Senators and Representatives to which the State may be entitled in the Congress; but no Senator or Representative, or person holding an office of trust or profit under the United States, shall be chosen an elector.

"The electors to which a State is entitled by virtue of its Senators shall be elected by the people thereof, and the electors to which it is entitled by virtue of its Representatives shall be elected by the people within single-elector districts established by the legislature thereof; such districts to be composed of compact and contiguous territory, containing as nearly as practicable the number of persons which entitled the State to one Representative in the Congress; and such districts when formed shall not be altered until another census has been taken. Before being chosen elector, each candidate for the office shall officially declare the persons for whom he will vote for President and Vice President, which declaration shall be binding on any successor. In choosing electors of President and Vice President the voters in each State shall have the qualifications requisite for electors of the most numerous branch of the State legislature, except that the legislature of any State may prescribe lesser qualifications with respect to residence therein.

"The electors shall meet in their respective States, fill any vacancies in their number as directed by the State legislature, and vote by signed ballot for President and Vice President, one of whom, at least, shall not be an inhabitant of the same State with themselves; they shall name in their ballots the person voted for as President, and in distinct ballots the person voted for as Vice President; and they shall make distinct lists of all persons voted for as President, and of all persons voted for as Vice President, and of the number of votes for each, excluding therefrom any votes for persons other than those named by an elector before he was chosen, unless one or both of the persons so named be deceased, which lists they shall sign and certify, and transmit sealed to the seat of government of the United States, directed to the President of the Senate; the President of the Senate shall, in the presence of the Senate and the House of Representatives, open all the certificates and the votes shall then be counted; the person having the greatest number of votes for President shall be the President, if such number be a majority of the whole number of electors chosen; and the person having the greatest number of votes for Vice President shall be the Vice President, if such a number be a majority of the whole number of electors chosen.

"If no person voted for as President has a majority of the whole number of electors, then from the persons having the three highest numbers on the lists of persons voted for as President, the

Senate and the House of Representatives, assembled and voting as individual Members of one body, shall choose immediately, by ballot, the President; a quorum for such purpose shall be three-fourths of the whole number of the Senators and Representatives, and a majority of the whole number shall be necessary to a choice; if additional ballots be necessary, the choice on the fifth ballot shall be between the two persons having the highest number of votes on the fourth ballot.

"If no person voted for as Vice President has a majority of the whole number of electors, then the Vice President shall be chosen from the persons having the three highest numbers on the lists of persons voted for as Vice President in the same manner as herein provided for choosing the President. But no person constitutionally ineligible to the office of President shall be eligible to that of Vice President of the United States.

"SEC. 2. The Congress may by law provide for the case of the death of any of the persons from whom the Senate and the House of Representatives may choose a President or a Vice President whenever the right of choice shall have devolved upon them.

"SEC. 3. This article supersedes the second and fourth paragraphs of section 1, article II, of the Constitution, the twelfth article of amendment to the Constitution and section 4 of the twentieth article of amendment to the Constitution. Except as herein expressly provided, this article does not supersede the twenty-third article of amendment.

"SEC. 4. Electors appointed pursuant to the twenty-third article of amendment to this Constitution shall be elected by the people of such district in such manner as the Congress may direct. Before being chosen as such elector, each candidate shall officially declare the persons for whom he will vote for President and Vice President, which declaration shall be binding on any successor. Such electors shall meet in the district and perform the duties provided in section 1 of this article.

"SEC. 5. This article shall take effect on the 1st day of July following its ratification."

APPENDIX IV

The Lodge-Gossett Plan
for Dividing the Electoral Vote of Each State
in Proportion to the Popular Vote,
as Revived by Senator John J. Sparkman
of Alabama,
and Three Other Senators

[S.J. Res. 84, 90th Cong., first sess.]

JOINT RESOLUTION Proposing an amendment to the Constitution
of the United States providing for the election of
President and Vice President

Resolved by the Senate and House of Representatives of the
United States of America in Congress assembled (two-thirds of
each House concurring therein), That an amendment is hereby
proposed to the Constitution of the United States, which shall be
valid to all intents and purposes as part of the Constitution only if
ratified by three-fourths of the legislatures of the several States
within seven years from the date of its submission by the Congress:

"ARTICLE —

"SECTION 1. The Executive power shall be vested in a President of the United States of America. He shall hold his office
during the term of four years, and, together with the Vice President, chosen for the same term, be elected as provided in this
Constitution.

"The office of elector of the President and Vice President, as
established by section 1 of article II and the twelfth article of

amendment to this Constitution, is hereby abolished. The President and Vice President shall be elected by the people of the several States and the District constituting the seat of government of the United States. The electors in each State shall have the qualifications requisite for electors of the most numerous branch of the State legislature, except that the legislature of any State may prescribe lesser qualifications with respect to residence therein. The electors in the District shall have such qualifications as the Congress may prescribe. The places and manner of holding such election in each State shall be prescribed by the legislature thereof; but the Congress may at any time by law make or alter such regulations. The place and manner of holding such election in the District shall be prescribed by the Congress. Congress shall determine the time of such election, which shall be the same throughout the United States. Until otherwise determined by the Congress, such election shall be held on the Tuesday next after the first Monday in November of the year preceding the year in which the regular term of the President is to begin. Each State shall be entitled to a number of electoral votes equal to the whole number of Senators and Representatives to which such State may be entitled in the Congress. The District shall be entitled to a number of electoral votes equal to the whole number of Senators and Representatives in Congress to which the District would be entitled if it were a State, but in no event more than the least populous State.

"Within forty-five days after such election, or at such time as Congress shall direct, the official custodian of the election returns of each State and the District shall make distinct lists of all persons for whom votes were cast for President and the number of votes for each, and the total vote of the electors of the State or the District for all persons for President, which lists he shall sign and certify and transmit sealed to the seat of the Government of the United States, directed to the President of the Senate. On the 6th day of January following the election, unless the Congress by law appoints a different day not earlier than the 4th day of January and not later than the 10th day of January, the President of the

Senate shall, in the presence of the Senate and House of Representatives, open all certificates and the votes shall then be counted. Each person for whom votes were cast for President in each State and the District shall be credited with such proportion of the electoral votes thereof as he received of the total vote of the electors therein for President. In making the computation, fractional numbers less than one one-thousandth shall be disregarded. The person having the greatest number of electoral votes for President shall be President, if such number be at least 40 per centum of the whole number of such electoral votes. If no person has at least 40 per centum of the whole number of electoral votes, then from the persons having the two highest number of electoral votes for President, the Senate and the House of Representatives sitting in joint session shall choose immediately, by ballot, the President. A majority of the votes of the combined authorized membership of the Senate and the House of Representatives shall be necessary for a choice.

"The Vice President shall be likewise elected, at the same time and in the same manner and subject to the same provisions, as the President, but no person constitutionally ineligible for the office of President shall be eligible to that of Vice President of the United States.

"The Congress may by law provide for the case of the death of any of the persons from whom the Senate and the House of Representatives may choose a President whenever the right of choice shall have devolved upon them, and for the case of death of any of the persons from whom the Senate and the House of Representatives may choose a Vice President whenever the right of choice shall have devolved upon them.

"Sec. 2. This article shall take effect on the 10th day of February next after one year shall have elapsed following its ratification."

APPENDIX V

The Johnson Administration Proposal
for Eliminating the Electoral College
as a Physical Entity
and Awarding the Total Electoral Vote
of Each State to the Winner of a Majority
or Plurality of the Popular Vote

The version printed in this appendix is a revision of the proposal as originally introduced. The revision was presented by the then Attorney General, Nicholas deB. Katzenbach, in behalf of the Johnson Administration. See *Election of the President,* Hearings Before the Subcommittee on Constitutional Amendments of the Senate Judiciary Committee, 89th Congress, 2nd Session (Washington, D.C., 1966), pp. 151, 160–162.

Suggested Revision of S.J. Res. 58

[S.J. Res. ——, 89th Cong., second sess.]

JOINT RESOLUTION Proposing an amendment to the Constitution
of the United States relating to the election of the
President and Vice President

Resolved by the Senate and House of Representatives of the United States of America in Congress assembled (two-thirds of each House concurring therein), That the following article is proposed as an amendment to the Constitution of the United States, which shall be valid to all intents and purposes as part of the Constitution when ratified by the legislatures of three-fourths of the several States within seven years from the date of its submission by the Congress:

"ARTICLE —

"SECTION 1. The President and the Vice President shall be elected as provided in this article. No person constitutionally

67

ineligible for the office of President shall be eligible for that of Vice President.

"SEC. 2. On the Tuesday next after the first Monday in November of the year preceding the year in which the regular term of the President is to begin, unless the Congress shall by law appoint a different day, there shall be held in each State and in the District of Columbia an election in which the people thereof shall cast their votes for President and for Vice President. In such election, each voter shall cast a single vote for two persons, one a candidate for President and the other a candidate for Vice-President, who shall have consented to the joining of their names on the ballot. The places and manner of holding the election shall be prescribed in each State by the legislature thereof but shall be subject to regulation by the Congress. The voters in each State shall have the qualifications requisite for persons voting for members of the most numerous branch of the State legislature. The voters in the District of Columbia shall have the qualifications prescribed by the Congress.

"There shall be cast for the persons receiving the greatest number of votes for President and for Vice President in each State a number of electoral votes equal to the whole number of Senators and Representatives to which that State may be entitled in the Congress. There shall be cast for the persons receiving the greatest number of votes for President and for Vice President in the District of Columbia a number of electoral votes equal to the whole number of Senators and Representatives to which the District would be entitled in the Congress if it were a State, but in no event more than the number cast by the least populous State.

"Within forty-five days after the election, or at such other times as the Congress may direct, the official custodian of the election returns of each State and of the District of Columbia shall prepare, sign, certify, and transmit sealed to the seat of the Government of the United States, directed to the President of the Senate, a list of all persons for whom votes were cast for President and a separate list of all persons for whom votes were cast for Vice

President. Upon each such list there shall be entered the number of votes cast for each person whose name appears thereon, the total number of votes cast for all such persons, and the name of the person for whom the electoral votes of such State or District are cast. . . ."

APPENDIX VI

The Bingham Proposal for a Runoff Election
Within the Electoral College System

[H.R.J. Res.——, 90th Cong., second sess.]

JOINT RESOLUTION Proposing an amendment to the Constitution
of the United States relating to the election of the
President and Vice President

*Resolved by the Senate and House of Representatives of the
United States of America in Congress assembled (two-thirds of
each House concurring therein),* That the following article is
proposed as an amendment to the Constitution of the United
States, which shall be valid to all intents and purposes as part of
the Constitution only if ratified by the legislatures of three-fourths
of the several States within seven years from the date of its submission by the Congress:

"ARTICLE —

"SECTION 1. In lieu of the method of election provided in section 1 of article II and in the twelfth and twentieth articles
of amendment, the President and Vice President shall be elected
as provided in this article.

"SEC. 2. Each State shall have a number of electoral votes for
President and Vice President equal to the whole number of
Senators and Representatives to which that State may be entitled
in the Congress. The places and manner of electing the President
and Vice President shall be prescribed by law in each State; but
the Congress may at any time by law prescribe the places and
manner of electing the President and Vice President.

"SEC. 3. The people of each State shall cast their votes for the
candidates for President and Vice President. The candidate for
President in each State receiving the greatest number of votes
shall receive that State's electoral votes for President, and the

candidate for Vice President in each State receiving the greatest number of votes for Vice President shall receive that State's electoral votes for Vice President.

"SEC. 4. The person receiving the greatest number of electoral votes for President, shall be President, if such number be a majority of the whole number of electoral votes; and the person receiving the greatest number of electoral votes for Vice President, shall be Vice President, if such number be a majority of the whole number of electoral votes.

"SEC. 5. If no person has a majority of the whole number of electoral votes for President or Vice President, there shall be a runoff election in which the names of the two persons with the greatest number of electoral votes for President or Vice President, as the case may be, shall appear on the ballot in each of the several States. The winner of such election shall be decided in the same manner as the election provided by sections 3 and 4 of this article.

"SEC. 6. The District constituting the seat of Government of the United States shall have a number of electoral votes equal to the whole number of Senators and Representatives in Congress to which the District would be entitled if it were a State, but in no event more than the least populous State.

"SEC. 7. The Congress may provide by law for the determination of any case affecting the election of the President or Vice President for which provision is not made by this article."

APPENDIX VII

The Johnson Administration Proposal
for Election by a Joint Session of Congress
in case of Deadlock

[S.J. Res. 58, 89th Cong., second sess.]
(Revised)

"SEC. 3. On the 6th day of January following the election, unless the Congress shall by law appoint a different day not earlier than the 4th day of January and not later than the 10th day of January, the President of the Senate shall, in the presence of the Senate and the House of Representatives, open all the certificates, and the electoral votes shall then be counted. The person having the greatest number of votes for President shall be the President, and the person having the greatest number of votes for Vice President shall be the Vice President, if such number be a majority of the whole number of electoral votes. If no person has a majority of the whole number of electoral votes for President or for Vice President, then from the three persons receiving the highest number of electoral votes for such office the Senate and the House of Representatives sitting in joint session shall immediately choose such officer by ballot. A quorum for this purpose shall consist of three-fourths of the whole number of the Senators and Representatives. The vote of each Member of each House shall be publicly announced and recorded, and in addition there shall be cast for the person for whom the electoral votes of the District of Columbia were cast a number of votes equal to the number of such electoral votes. The person receiving the greatest number of votes shall be chosen.

"SEC. 4. If, at the time fixed for the counting of the electoral votes as provided in section 3, the person who would have been entitled to receive a majority of the electoral votes for President shall have died, the person who is entitled to receive the majority of the electoral votes for Vice President shall be President.

"The Congress may by law provide for the case of the death of any of the persons for whom the Senate and the House of Representatives may choose a President or a Vice President whenever the right of choice shall have devolved upon them; for the case of the death of both the persons who, except for their death, would have been entitled to become President and Vice President; and for the case of the death or withdrawal, prior to the election provided for in section 2, of a candidate for President or for Vice President.

SEC. 5. The Congress shall have power to enforce this article by appropriate legislation."

APPENDIX VIII

Proposal for a National Presidential Primary Election,
Offered by
Senators Margaret Chase Smith, Republican of Maine,
and George Aiken, Republican of Vermont

Further sections of this resolution, which would abolish the electoral college and establish the direct popular election of Presidents, are omitted.

[S.J. Res. 6, 90th Cong., first sess.]

JOINT RESOLUTION Proposing an amendment to the Constitution of the United States providing for nomination of candidates for President and Vice President, and for election of such candidates by popular vote

Resolved by the Senate and House of Representatives of the United States of America in Congress assembled (two-thirds of each House concurring therein), That the following article is proposed as an amendment to the Constitution of the United States, which shall be valid for all intents and purposes as part of the Constitution when ratified by the legislatures of three-fourths of the several States:

"ARTICLE —

"SECTION 1. The executive power shall be vested in a President of the United States of America. He shall hold his office during the term of four years and, together with the Vice President, chosen for the same term, be nominated and elected as hereinafter provided.

"SEC. 2. The official candidates of political parties for President and Vice President shall be nominated at a primary election by direct popular vote. Voters in each State shall have the qualifications requisite for electors of the most numerous branch of the State legislature, but, in the primary election each voter shall be eligible to vote only in the primary of the party of his registered affiliation. The time of such primary election shall be the same throughout the United States, and, unless the Congress shall by law appoint a different day, such primary election shall be held on the first Tuesday after the first Monday in August in the year preceding the expiration of the regular term of President and Vice President. No person shall be a candidate for nomination for President or Vice President except in the primary of the party of his registered affiliation, and his name shall be on that party's ballot in all the States if he shall have filed a petition at the seat of the Government of the United States with the Secretary of State, which petition shall be valid only if (1) it is determined by the Secretary of State to have been signed on or after the first day of January of the year in which the next primary election for President and Vice President is to be held by a number of qualified voters, in any or all of the several States, equal in number to at least 1 per centum, but not more than 2 per centum, of the total number of popular votes cast throughout the United States for all candidates for President (or, in the case of the primary election first held after the ratification of this article, for electors of President and Vice President) in the most recent previous presidential election, and (2) it is filed with the Secretary of State not later than the first Tuesday after the first Monday in June of the year in which the next primary election for President and Vice President is to be held. No person's name shall appear on the ballot in any primary election as a candidate for nomination for both President and Vice President; but the foregoing shall not, except in the case of a runoff election, prohibit the name of a candidate for nomination for President, or the name of any other person, from being written on the ballot by the voters for nomination for Vice President, or the name of a candidate for nomination for Vice President, or the name of any other person, from being written on the ballot by the voters for nomination for President.

"Sec. 3. For the purposes of this article a political party shall be recognized as such if at any time within four years next preceding a primary election the Secretary of State determines such party has had registered as members thereof more than 5 per centum of the total registered voters in the United States.

"Sec. 4. Within fifteen days after such primary election, the chief executive of each State shall make distinct lists of all persons of each political party for whom votes were cast, and the number of votes for each such person, which lists shall be signed, certified, and transmitted under the seal of such State to the seat of the Government of the United States directed to the Secretary of State, who shall forthwith open all certificates and count the votes. The person receiving a majority of the total number of popular votes cast for presidential nominees by the voters of the party of his registered affiliation shall be the official candidate of such party for President throughout the United States, and the person receiving a majority of the total number of popular votes cast for vice-presidential nominees by the voters of the party of his registered affiliation shall be the official candidate of such party for Vice President throughout the United States. If no person receives a majority of the total number of popular votes cast for presidential nominees by the voters of a political party, a runoff election to determine the nominee of such political party for President shall be conducted throughout the United States on the twenty-eighth day after the day on which the primary election was held. Such runoff election shall be between the two persons who received the greatest number of popular votes cast for presidential nominees by the voters of such political party in the primary election. If no person receives a majority of the total number of popular votes cast for vice-presidential nominees by the voters of a political party, a runoff election to determine the nominee of such political party for Vice President shall be conducted throughout the United States on the twenty-eighth day after the day on which the primary election was held. Such runoff election shall be between the two persons who received the greatest number of popular votes cast for vice-presidential nominees by the voters of such political party in the primary election. No person ineligible to vote in the primary election of any political party shall be eligible to vote in a runoff election of such political party. Within fifteen days after a runoff election for the nomination of a political party for President or Vice President, the chief executive of each State shall, in the case of a runoff election for nomination for President, transcribe on an appropriate document the names of the two persons on the party's ballot for nomination for President and the number of votes cast in such State for each, and, in the case of a runoff election for nomination for Vice President, transcribe on an appropriate document the names of the two persons on the party's ballot for nomination for Vice President and the number of votes cast in such State for each, which documents shall be signed, certified, and transmitted under the seal of such State to the seat of the Government of the United States, directed to the Secretary of State, who shall forthwith open all certificates and count the votes. The person receiving the majority of popular votes for President in a runoff election to elect a nominee for President shall be the official candidate of such political party for President throughout the United States. The person receiving the majority of popular votes for Vice President in a runoff election to elect a nominee for Vice President shall be the official candidate of such political party for Vice President throughout the United States.

"Sec. 5. In the event a person shall receive in any such primary election, as the result of write-in votes, a majority of the total number of votes cast by the voters of the party of his registered affiliation for nominees for President and a majority of the total number of votes cast by such voters for nominees for Vice President, such person shall declare which nomination he accepts; and a runoff election shall be conducted for the nomination such person does not accept between the two persons who received the next highest number of votes for such nomination.

"In the event a person shall receive in any such primary election, as the result of write-in votes, the highest or second highest number of votes cast by the voters of the party of his registered affiliation for nominees for President (and no person receives a majority) and the highest or second highest number of votes cast by such voters for nominees for Vice President (and no person receives a majority), such person shall declare the office for which he will be a candidate in the runoff election provided for in section 4 of this article and such person may not be a candidate for nomination for the other office. The runoff election for the nomination for such other office shall be between the two persons who received the next highest number of votes for such other office.

"In the event a person shall receive in any such primary election, as the result of write-in votes, a majority of the total number of votes cast by the voters of the party of his registered affiliation for nominees for President and the highest or second highest number of votes cast by such voters for nominees for Vice President (and no person receives a majority), or such person receives a majority of the total number of votes cast for nominees for Vice President and the highest or second highest number of votes cast for nominees for President (and no person receives a majority), such person may, in either such case, accept a nomination for the office for which he received a majority of the votes cast, and a runoff election shall be conducted for the other office between the two persons who received the next highest number of votes for such office; or, such person may refuse the nomination for the office for which he received a majority of the votes cast and declare himself a candidate in the runoff election provided for in section 4 of this article for the office for which he received the highest or second highest number of votes. If such person refuses the nomination for an office for which he received a majority of the votes cast, a runoff election shall be conducted for such office between the two persons who received the next highest number of votes for such office. Any runoff election provided for in this section shall be conducted at the same time, and the results thereof certified in the same manner, as provided for runoff elections under section 4 of this article.

"If, in any case in which a runoff election would otherwise be held, only one candidate of a party remains for nomination for President or Vice President, as the case may be, such candidate shall be the official candidate of such party for such office and no runoff election shall be conducted for such office.

"Sec. 6. In the event of the death or resignation of the official candidate of any political party for President, the person nominated by such political party for Vice President shall be the official candidate of such party for President. In the event of the deaths or resignations of the official candidates of any political party for President and Vice President, or in the event of the death or resignation of the official candidate of any political party for Vice President, a national committee of such party shall designate such candidate or candidates, who shall then be deemed the official candidate or candidates of such party, but in choosing such candidate or candidates the vote shall be taken by States, the delegation from each State having one vote. A quorum for such purposes shall consist of a delegate or delegates from two-thirds of the States, and a majority of all States shall be necessary to a choice. . . ."

APPENDIX IX

Recommendation by the
United States Civil Rights Commission of Action
to Ban Racial Discrimination
*by Political Parties**

THE NATIONAL *political parties should take immediate steps to*
require State political party organizations, as a precondition to the
seating of their delegations at their national conventions, to—

(1) eliminate all vestiges of discrimination at every level
of party activity including primary elections, meetings, and conventions, and the election and appointment of party officials;

(2) publicize fully, in such manner as to assure adequate
notice to all interested parties (a) the time and place
of all public meetings of the party at every level, in
places accessible to, and large enough to accom-
modate, all party members; (b) a full description of
the legal and practical procedures for selection of
party officers and representatives at every level; and
(c) a full description of the legal and practical
qualifications for all officers and representatives of
the party at every level; and

(3) take affirmative steps to open activities to all party
members regardless of race.

Prompt action by the national political parties before and at
their forthcoming conventions could obviate the need for legisla-
tion by Congress to establish specific guidelines covering the
activities of political parties to assure the accomplishment of these
objectives.

* United States Commission on Civil Rights, *Political Participation*
(Washington, D.C., Government Printing Office, 1968), pp. 187–188.

APPENDIX X

Call for the 1968 Democratic National Convention

January 9, 1968

TO WHOM IT MAY CONCERN:

By authority of the Democratic National Committee, the National Convention of the Democratic Party is hereby called to meet in the International Amphitheatre, West 43rd and Halsted Streets, Chicago, Illinois, on the 26th day of August, 1968, at an hour to be determined at a later date for the purpose of selecting nominees for President and Vice President of the United States of America, to adopt and promulgate a platform and to take such other action with respect to any other matters as the Convention may deem advisable.

Notice is hereby given that the following resolutions have been approved by the Democratic National Committee with recommendation that they be adopted as rules applicable to the 1968 Democratic National Convention. . . .

The basis for the foregoing [see table, pp. 82-3] distribution of votes, delegates and alternates is the resolution adopted by the Democratic National Committee on January 8, 1968, which reads as follows:

(1) Each State shall have three (3) Convention votes for each of the Electors from that State in the Electoral College.

(2) Each State shall have a popular vote bonus equal to one Convention vote for each 100,000 popular votes, or major fraction thereof, cast in that State in 1964 for Electors who either voted for the nominees of the 1964 Democratic National Convention or who were not elected but ran on the ticket of voting for said nominees provided that there shall be a minimum of one such bonus vote for each State.

(3) There shall be a victory bonus of ten (10) Convention

The distribution of votes, delegates and alternates for said

State	A 1968 Convention Vote	B Nat'l. Comm. Members*	C Maximum No.** of Delegates to be selected (From Cols. 2E and 2D)		D Maximum No. of Alternates to be Selected	E Maximum Total*** Delegation
Alabama	32	2	# 56 with	30 votes	30	88
Alaska	22	2	20 "	20 "	20	42
Arizona	19	2	# 32 "	17 "	17	51
Arkansas	33	2	# 52 "	31 "	31	85
California	174	2	172 "	172 "	172	346
Colorado	35	2	# 40 "	33 "	33	75
Connecticut	44	2	42 "	42 "	42	86
Delaware	22	2	20 "	20 "	20	42
Florida	63	2	61 "	61 "	61	124
Georgia	43	2	64 "	41 "	41	107
Hawaii	26	2	24 "	24 "	24	50
Idaho	25	2	# 24 "	23 "	23	49
Illinois	118	2	#136 "	116 "	116	254
Indiana	63	2	# 66 "	61 "	61	129
Iowa	46	2	# 50 "	44 "	44	96
Kansas	38	2	# 40 "	36 "	36	78
Kentucky	46	2	# 60 "	44 "	44	106
Louisiana	36	2	# 50 "	34 "	34	86
Maine	27	2	# 28 "	25 "	25	55
Maryland	49	2	47 "	47 "	47	96
Massachusetts	72	2	# 80 "	70 "	70	152
Michigan	96	2	#100 "	94 "	94	196
Minnesota	52	2	# 60 "	50 "	50	112
Mississippi	24	2	# 44 "	22 "	22	68
Missouri	60	2	# 76 "	58 "	58	136
Montana	26	2	# 30 "	24 "	24	56
Nebraska	30	2	# 30 "	28 "	28	60
Nevada	22	2	# 28 "	20 "	20	50
New Hampshire	26	2	24 "	24 "	24	50
New Jersey	82	2	80 "	80 "	80	162
New Mexico	26	2	# 32 "	24 "	24	58

DELEGATES AND ALTERNATES

1968 Democratic National Convention shall be as follows:

State	A 1968 Convention Vote	B Nat'l Comm. Members*	C Maximum No.** of Delegates to be selected (From Cols. 2E and 2D)			D Maximum No. of Alternates to be Selected	E Maximum Total*** Delegation
New York	190	2	#226	with	188 votes	188	416
North Carolina	59	2	# 72	"	57 "	57	131
North Dakota	25	2	23	"	23 "	23	48
Ohio	115	2	#126	"	113 "	113	241
Oklahoma	41	2	# 56	"	39 "	39	97
Oregon	35	2	33	"	33 "	33	68
Pennsylvania	130	2	#160	"	128 "	128	290
Rhode Island	27	2	# 32	"	25 "	25	59
South Carolina	28	2	# 40	"	26 "	26	68
South Dakota	26	2	24	"	25 "	24	50
Tennessee	51	2	# 64	"	49 "	49	115
Texas	104	2	#120	"	102 "	102	224
Utah	26	2	24	"	24 "	24	50
Vermont	22	2	20	"	20 "	20	42
Virginia	54	2	# 64	"	52 "	52	118
Washington	47	2	# 52	"	45 "	45	99
West Virginia	38	2	# 48	"	36 "	36	86
Wisconsin	59	2	# 60	"	57 "	57	119
Wyoming	22	2	# 26	"	20 "	20	48
Dist. of Columbia	23	2	21	"	21 "	21	44
Canal Zone	5	2	# 6	"	3 "	3	11
Guam	5	2	# 6	"	3 "	3	11
Puerto Rico	8	2	# 12	"	6 "	6	20
Virgin Islands	5	2	# 6	"	3 "	3	11
TOTALS	2622	110	2989	"	2512 "	2512	5611

* Each National Committee member has an automatic vote within his delegation; no alternates may be substituted.

** Excludes National Committee members.

*** Includes National Committee members.

votes for each State which cast its Electoral votes for the nominees of the 1964 Democratic National Convention.

(4) Each member of the Democratic National Committee elected by the 1964 Democratic National Convention or subsequent thereto by the Democratic National Committee shall have one Convention vote, said vote to be personal and to be incapable of exercise by any alternate.

(5) Canal Zone, Guam, Puerto Rico and the Virgin Islands shall have twenty-three (23) Convention votes, inclusive of the votes of members of the Democratic National Committee, distributed as follows:

Canal Zone	5
Guam	5
Puerto Rico	8
Virgin Islands	5

FURTHER RESOLVED, that in selecting individuals to cast Convention votes other than the votes of members of the Democratic National Committee, each State shall select a delegate for each vote and an alternate for each vote, except that a State shall be entitled to select the same number of individuals to serve as delegates as it was authorized to select for the 1964 Democratic National Convention, and if such number of individual delegates exceeds the number of Convention votes authorized for delegates selected by the State then fractional votes (consisting of one-half vote per delegate) may be assigned to the extent necessary, provided that this exception shall not apply to alternates.

FURTHER RESOLVED, that the allocation of votes, whether on a Congressional district, at-large or other basis, shall be determined within each State, it being recommended that, to the extent permitted by State law, consideration be given to the foregoing principles underlying the determination of National Convention votes and equitable allowances provided on the basis thereof.

JOHN M. BAILEY, Chairman
Democratic National Committee

COLOPHON BOOKS ON POLITICAL SCIENCE

*In Preparation